The
Identity
Driven
Life

Eddymufy A. Eyienyien

Paperback: 978-1-967820-13-9
eBook: 978-1-967820-14-6
Library of Congress Control Number: 2025908236

This is a work of nonfiction.

Ordering Information:

Prime Seven Media
518 Landmann St.
Tomah City, WI 54660

Printed in the United States of America

Foreword

Hailing from a humble village in the heart of southwest Nigeria, Eddymufy is more than just someone I know—he is family, bound not just by blood but by life itself. His journey, like that of many, began in uncertainty, yet it was shaped by an unshakable determination to rise beyond circumstances, discover purpose, and embrace the truth of who he is.

Life is not merely about movement—it is about direction. To be driven is more than just traveling from point A to point B; it is about walking a path with intention, guided by a deeper understanding of identity. If your destination is a thousand miles away, each step forward, no matter how small, is a step toward self-discovery. Often, we assume we know who we are, yet true identity is not found in assumptions but in exploration, courage, and clarity.

Many of us struggle with the question: *Who am I?* Society tells us one thing, expectations another, and our fears yet another. In this chaos, it is easy to lose sight of our essence.

But identity is not just a name, a title, or a background—it is the foundation of everything we are and aspire to be. When we understand ourselves, our choices become purposeful, our paths clearer, and our goals within reach.

This book is a call to action—an invitation to rediscover yourself. It challenges you to reflect deeply, to shed self-doubt, and to embrace a journey of self-awareness. As the saying goes, while we may not choose where we come from, we have the power to determine where we end up. The future is not a distant reality; it is being shaped right now, in this moment, by how well we use today.

From the very beginning of humanity, identity has been central to our existence. Before the fall, identity was clear, untainted. Yet, throughout history, mankind has struggled to reclaim it. We chase definitions given to us by others, seeking validation in places that only lead us further away from our truth. But identity is not something to be *found*—it is something to be *understood*.

This book is more than just words on a page; it is a guide, a mirror, and a map. It will challenge you, inspire you, and lead you toward a deeper understanding of yourself. As you read, open your mind and heart. Let each chapter be a step forward in your journey toward clarity, purpose, and a life lived with intention. Because the greatest discovery you will ever make is not in the world around you—but within yourself.

-Wilson Okosun

Pastor

Acknowledgments

To my three amazing children, Sky, Star, and Eagle, thank you for your patience, your understanding, and your unwavering love. Sky, your constant help in keeping the little ones at bay when I needed to focus was invaluable. I truly don't know how I would have managed without your steady presence and willingness to step in whenever I needed you. Star and Eagle, your cooperation, your laughter, and your boundless energy made this writing journey so much smoother. You each brought me joy, even in the most challenging moments, and reminded me why perseverance is always worth it. I love you kidos beyond words, and I am endlessly proud to be your dad.

To my dear friend, Leticia, I owe you a debt of gratitude that words can't fully express. You've been more than just a support system; you've been a lifeline. I can't count the number of times I've accidentally deleted entire versions of this manuscript—permanently deleted, even from the trash!—and your incredible IT skills have saved me time and time again. Your patience in dealing with my tech mishaps was nothing short of saintly, and your encouragement never wavered. Beyond the technical rescues, your constant check-ins, your reminders to breathe, and your unwavering belief in me kept me pushing forward, even when I felt like giving up. You held me accountable, cheered me on, and sometimes even nudged me past my own excuses. I am beyond grateful for your friendship and support, and I could not have done this without you.

To all my friends who have been part of this journey, thank you from the depths of my heart. Your kindness, stories, wisdom, and unwavering encouragement have meant more to me than words can express. Whether you offered a quiet word of motivation, celebrated my progress, or simply gave me the space to focus during the long and often grueling hours of writing, you have each left an undeniable imprint on this book and on my heart.

Writing a book is often seen as a solitary endeavor, but in truth, it is shaped by the support, patience, and love of those who walk alongside the writer. To those who have tirelessly championed this project, who have believed in its worth even before it came to life, and who have waited with patience and anticipation—your faith in me and in this book has been a source of strength. Your messages and calls, asking when it would finally be available, were not just inquiries; they were powerful reminders that this story mattered, that it had a place in the world, and that I was not alone in bringing it to life.

Though I may not have been able to name each of you individually in these pages, please know that your presence has been deeply felt in every chapter, every word, and every moment of this journey. I carry my gratitude for you always, and this book stands as a testament to the love and encouragement that have lifted me along the way.

With deep appreciation and love, Eddymufy

Table of Contents

CHAPTER 1

The power of time!

By the time I truly understood what my life was all about, son, I realized there wasn't much time left to live it. Those were the last words of Mr. Bent—words that have stayed with me ever since, shaping how I see life and time.

It was a quiet Sunday morning when I called my friend, Mikel, to pick me up so we could visit his father together at the hospital. I didn't know Mr. Bent very well, but in the short time I spent with him, he left a deep impression. Growing up without a father and being rejected by my father, I always felt like something was missing. Watching Bent and Mikel together made me see what I had lost and what I had always wished for.

When we walked into the hospital room, the first thing I noticed wasn't Mr. Bent himself. It was the sound of the life-support machine—a steady, rhythmic beep. It was haunting, like a reminder that time was running out. Only after hearing that sound did I look at the man in the bed.

Bent had always been known as funny and hardworking, but now he looked weak and helpless, hooked up to machines. My chest felt tight just looking at him. He had been diagnosed with a terminant heart condition—I can't remember the name—but the details didn't matter. What mattered was the pain on his face and the love in his eyes as he looked at Mikel.

I stood there with my arms crossed, feeling helpless as Bent held Mikel's hand tightly. His knuckles turned white, as if he was holding on to every last bit of strength he had. Even in that moment, there was so much love in his Look. He shifted his head slightly on the pillow and, with labored breaths, began to speak.

Son, he said, his voice soft but full of feeling. use your time wisely. By the time I figured out what really mattered, it was too late to do much about it. Take care of your health, Make peace with your brother. Keep your family close. And don't let your dreams stay dreams, make sure you turn them into reality. Life is not meant to simply dream, but to live them out. It's a gift, son, one that you unwrap slowly, day by day. Tears burned in my eyes, but I held them back. I wanted to be strong for Mikel, yet inside, I was unraveling. We spend so much of our lives stressing over work deadlines, financial struggles, social dramas, and trivial inconveniences. But as the saying goes, We all have 99 problems until we get sick—then we have only one. As I stood and watched Mike helplessly, this wasn't just a saying I have read or heard someone one says anymore, it was a reality playing out right before my eyes.

Illness has a way of stripping everything down to its essence. Standing there, watching the once-powerful and always-busy Mr. Bent lying helpless in that hospital bed, I was struck by a painful truth—health is not something we should chase when it's slipping away; it's something we must protect while we still have it. Yet, ironically, we are often frugal in maintaining our health but willing to spend everything, our savings, our energy, even borrowed time, when we realize too late that it's slipping from our grasp. That moment taught me a lesson I will never forget: nothing truly matters if we don't have our health. And by the time we're forced to prioritize it, we may have already lost too much.

I left that hospital room with Mr. Bent's words echoing in my heart, like a guide to living better. Even now, when I feel lost or rushed, I hear his voice reminding me—time is a gift, and it's up to us to use it well.

Every day, we are surrounded by countless opportunities, but we often fail to see them clearly. As the French- Cuban Americans writer Anais Nin once said, we don't see things as they are; we see them as we are. Identity crisis often overclowed our vision and makes us view opportunities as problems instead of recognizing their potential. One important lesson I've learned is this: life changes and takes on new trajectory, when we start to face situations with honesty, and see things for what they truly are, not just how they seem.

I've also realized something about time that we often don't truly value it the way we should, and as result of this, we are rarely intentional about how quickly it slips away from us. We often don't even notice it disappearing until it's too late. We stress over minor financial losses, fretting about every penny spent or misplaced. We guard our replaceable possessions, hesitating to share or lend them, fearing they might be lost or damaged. Yet, paradoxically, we let our most irreplaceable resource, our time, slip through our fingers without hesitation or a second thought.

True wisdom lies in understanding the value of what can't be replaced. time is a non refundable commodity, stay intentional while spending it.

Not long ago, I had a court hearing with my ex-wife at 1:15 PM to discuss custody of our children. That morning, I had work to finish, and as the deadline approached, I rushed to ensure I arrived on time. In the midst of this pressure, something interesting happened—I ignored calls, filtered distractions, and focused only on what I thought truly mattered. I was determined not to let anything make me late.

At that moment, a quiet inner voice asked: *What if you lived your whole life with this kind of focus and purpose? What if you managed your time as wisely as you are right now?* That thought hit me hard. Time is finite, it's our most limited resource.

It made me realize that time is like a ticket to the grand show of life. You can use your ticket to take the stage and perform—expressing your passion, creativity, and hard work—or you can sit in the audience, watching others perform and take the credit. To truly honor the gift of time, we must choose to step up as performers, making the most of every moment we're given.

During a vacation in the beautiful city of Florence, Italy, I stumbled upon an abandoned Lamborghini. It was rusted, forgotten, and covered in dust—its shine and value hidden. This reminded me of how many of us let our time and potential go to waste, unused and unappreciated. Like that car, we were made for greatness, but we must choose to take care of what we've been given and use it to its fullest.

allure faded. i coudn't help but wonder—how did it end up like this? Once a symbol of luxury and pride, now reduced to an artifact of disuse. What happened? The answer: time. Time is one of the most profound forces in existence, shaping lives, legacies, and entire landscapes without ever announcing its presence. It wears down mountains, crumbles empires, and redefines what we consider priceless. In its silent march, it gives and takes, often without us noticing until the change is beyond reversal. And yet, in its hands, lies one of the greatest gifts we can receive: the opportunity to fight for what matters to us. I want you to take a moment to reflect on people you've seen change over time. Maybe the once energetic and very active people you know have over the time become weak and humble, or the desolate, barren lands you once knew have blossomed into thriving communities having all the most beautiful structures erected on it. Time is an equalizer; it reshapes the world, constantly rewriting stories in a way that we can't always predict. But here's the thing—time is also a battlefield where everyone who is placed on it has to constantly fight for what we want or get overwhelmed by what we don't want. It's a space granted to each of us, to create, build, and strive for the lives we desire. How we use this space is what determines the outcome of our story. we have to fight—not against time itself, but against every force, behaviours and attitudes that is trying or has masqueraded our identity. Against a mindset that keeps busy telling you to settle for an ordinary being. Picture yourself five years from now, and you are looking back with pride, knowing you did not give in to the temptation and deception of simply existing, or being a spectator in someone else's dream. This is a fight about rejecting and removing the mask covering your true identity. It's saying no to a life where you only watch others be, do and achieve the things you secretly desire for yourself. Like my grandmother will always say, I only see the clothes I would have loved to wear on others, and so it was till she passed away. It's a simple statement that literally has nothing to do with a piece of clothes, but an unbearable agony of unlived life. a powerful one, a reminder to pursue one's dreams and destiny, instead of admiring beautiful life only on others, and writing yourself off of the possibility of being and having. The belief that being great and doing great things is only for some certain class of people is like a terminal virus that may not often be able trace how and or when it slides into our thinking system, but only start seeing the effect that it's leading us to doubt not just our own potential only, but also the accomplishments of those around us. Before i forget, let me quickly remind you of this, keep alert of the inner storm that rages lie within- constantly saying, I am the worst in here, I do not deserve this, this is meant for others not me, i don't belong here, but they do. I am not good enough for this. You are a special human. You are more than these lies, You are a reflection of the divine. The light of the world, salt of the earth, God's beloved child And more. When you are aware of your inheritage and potential, you not only lift yourself, but inspire others to do the same. It's about shining in a way that liberates, rather than intimidates. Few things in life are as painful as realizing you're off-track in life. that the road you are traveling was never your journey, that the life you are living is a mask-on and was never the life meant for you. Most especially if you are strained or feeling empty and frustrated. the moment that you begin to get this awakening, it's a signal to put yourself up and get ready to fight for something more meaningful. a fight to regain your identity and mission. Confucius once said, We have two lives, and the second begins when we realize we only have one. Recognizing this truth is a wake-up call—it's an invitation to begin turning your frustration into a journey toward transformation. The ultimate truth is that the cost of ignoring our potential is way far beyond what we can mentally and logically phattom. starting from personal unfilfiment, financial losses, emotional cost, opportunity losses, physical body and mental health jeopardy, social cost, and many more. The cumulative effect of ignoring our potential is a total disaster. to begin changing the tragetory of your life, taking the mask off, and fing finding your route in life, you must begin to understand what success means to you. otherwise you may soon find yourself from one wrong road to another wrong path. remember, success is relative, what it means to may not be what means to another. know what it means to you. begin setting attainable steps, invest in your development, take risks, seek help when needed and take responsibility for your life. This transformation project starts with renewing your mind, to begin the journey of being born again. Breaking free from limiting beliefs from a wrong identity, and embracing new perspectives that will give you the power to reshape your reality. Take a closer look at the life you've created. Which parts of it bring you satisfaction, and which parts weigh you down? In every situation of dissatisfaction—whether in finances, health, relationships, or personal satisfaction—there's often a disconnect between what we desire and the paths we've taken. Desires are like destinations; they require a specific direction. There is always a road that leads to every desire. If you wish to reach the east coast but find yourself heading to the north pole, you'll never arrive at your intended destination. Insufficiency is never always a shortage of resources or opportunities but stem from both intentional and unintentional misalignment of efforts.

Within each of us is an energy source that connects us to our desires, but for it to flow effectively, we need to align ourselves with it. This energy is the divine spark within, capable of manifesting our dreams if we give it permission. I remembered my grandmother always said that if you hold life very well, it's never heavy, but if you don't, it's like a heavy rock. It's not really the life we live that is hard, it's often how we live that makes it hard.

Saying life is easy to the hearing of someone who is struggling might sound dismissive, or even offensive. Life's challenges vary for everyone, and no two people face the same circumstances or hurdles. But there's truth in the idea that life is as easy—or as difficult—as we believe it to be. He who said life is hard and he who said life is easy are actually equally right. I remember when I was first learning to drive a car, and my instructor insisting it was easy was frustrating beyond words. For him, it was simple; for me, it was an overwhenming challenge. Yet, once I learned, I understood what he meant that it's easy

Life often feels overwhelming when we're still trying to figure things out, doesn't it? When we don't yet have the right perspective or haven't learned what really matters, everything feels heavier. But as we grow, some things start to make sense. One of the biggest lessons I've learned is that when we focus on serving others with our unique gifts and talents, life starts to feel more meaningful. It's like we're connecting to something deeper than ourselves. That's why the words in Matthew 23:11 resonate so much: The greatest among you will be your servant. Real greatness isn't about collecting accolades or achievements; it's about showing up for others in ways that uplift and inspire them.

But here's the truth: living with purpose and serving others isn't always easy. It takes courage. And I don't mean courage like being fearless in the face of danger—I mean the kind of courage it takes to stop caring so much about what other people think of you. To stand in your truth and shine your light, even if it makes others uncomfortable. One of the best pieces of advice I've ever heard is this: never mess with someone who has nothing to lose. There's something so powerful about that idea—when you let go of the fear of failing or being judged, no one can control you. You're free.

Let me ask you this: how many of us are trapped, not by actual walls, but by the fear of what people will say or think? It's the most crowded prison in the world, and most of us are in it without realizing. We hesitate, we hold back, and we second-guess ourselves because we're so scared of being misunderstood or criticized. But here's the thing: when you live like that, you're not really living. As I once read, "A man who doesn't fear failure, loss, or effort can never truly be defeated." And I believe that. When we let go of those fears, we start to feel lighter. We stop trying to be everything to everyone, and we become who we were always meant to be.

If there's one thing I've learned, it's this: life is too short to let fear hold us back. Discover who you are. Invest in that person. Share your gifts with the world. Not everyone will understand you, and that's okay. What matters is that you live authentically, boldly, and without regret. Because at the end of the day, the people who matter will see you for who you are, and the rest? They were never meant to stay anyway.

To truly find freedom, there are three steps I believe we all need to take: discover who you really are, invest in developing and nurturing that identity, and then share it with the world. These steps don't just change how you see yourself—they change how the world responds to you. Without them, so many people spend their lives feeling empty, living as spectators instead of creators, admiring what others have achieved but never stepping into their own potential.

Let me share something personal. My grandmother was one of the most remarkable women I've ever known, but I watched her spend much of her life admiring the beautiful life others had, wishing for things she never allowed herself to have. It wasn't just sad—it broke my heart. To me, it's a terrible disaster to live your life as only a consumer, someone who takes in the world but never contributes anything meaningful back to it. That's no way to live.

Here's the truth: your life has value, and your gifts—your skills, your strengths, even your kindness—are meant to be shared. Your wealth isn't just in your bank account and the stuff you have; it's in the lives you touch and the experiences you create for others. Think about it: so much of what we spend your money on comes from someone else's effort, skill, or creativity. So ask yourself, *what can I offer to the world?* What is your unique contribution, something others would also invest money and time in, too?

I believe we're all creators at our core. The Bible even describes creation as God's way of expressing Himself—He created the heavens, the earth, and everything in between. And if we're made in His image, doesn't that mean we're meant to create too? Not just to produce but to nurture, to build something that lasts. When we spend our lives only consuming—whether it's things, experiences, or even ideas—we miss out on the true joy of life: creating, giving, and sharing.

Think of it this way: the world is like a marketplace. There are two types of people that show up every day: those who show up with their skills and those who show up with their needs. Which side are you on? Take a moment—use your tongue to count your teeth, as the saying goes. Are you bringing something valuable to the table, or are you only taking from it?

I know finding your place in the world isn't always easy. True happiness comes when you find your work, your *real* work. The kind of work that lights you up inside and makes you feel alive. It's not just about money or status; it's about purpose. It's about waking up every morning with a sense of excitement, knowing that what you're doing matters. And yes, jobs can be great—they pay the bills, they help us grow, they teach us discipline. But a job and your life's work aren't always the same thing.

I've often seen people ridicule 9-to-5 kinds of jobs as if they're traps or just ways to survive, and I get it. I've even read articles where jobs and salary are being compared to drugs handed out by employers to keep you distracted from your dreams. But I don't agree with that. Sure, your job might not be your ultimate calling, but it serves a purpose. It's there to sustain you, to keep you going while you figure things out.

In 2017, I had the chance to interview Rasmus Lindgren on *The Impact Talk Show*. I asked him, What advice would you give to people who are still working 9-to-5 jobs? His answer was simple, but it stuck with me: *Happily keep your job while you're figuring out who you are.* And you know what? He was right. Too often, we're told to take a leap or chase our passions at all costs, but that advice can sometimes lead to disaster if we're not ready. Quitting without a plan or a sense of who you are can leave you lost and desperate. As Rasmus said, motivation is a double-edged sword—it can either push you toward wisdom or lead you astray.

Think of your job like a life raft. It's not where you're meant to stay forever, but it's vital while you're crossing rough waters. It keeps you afloat while you work on building the boat that will take you further. Your job is there to support you, not define you. When you understand that, you'll see it differently. You'll appreciate it, even if it's not your dream job, because it's part of the journey to something greater.

But here's the thing: don't let yourself get too comfortable that you feel at home where God simply wants you to take some rest. Jobs, like rest stops, serve a purpose, but they're not the destination. The saddest thing is when we stay in situations—whether it's a job, a relationship, or an environment—that no longer serves us because we are often afraid of change. As Carl Jung once said, The greatest tragedy of the family is the unlived life of the parent. Imagine that. The dreams we bury, the potential we waste, and the purpose we ignore don't just die with us—they become legacies of regret that we pass down to the next generation.

So, here's my suggestion to you: don't settle. Don't let fear or comfort keep you from discovering who you are and sharing that with the world. Use your job as a stepping stone, not a destination. And above all, find your work—your calling, the thing that makes you feel alive and joyful. Nurture it.

Prioritize it. And when the time is right, step fully into it. Because that's where true freedom and fulfillment live.

Self-love is at the heart of breaking free. Far too many people compromise their happiness by staying where they feel small, unfulfilled, or stifled. Every moment spent in an unhappy space is time borrowed against your potential. And time is not an infinite resource. Every day, the clock ticks forward, moving you either closer to fulfillment or farther from it. Time is the most powerful asset you have, be wise with it.

If you know who you are, you enter every space with a quiet confidence. As Maya Angelou said, You enter a room with a certain authority—not because you ask for it, but because you know you have it. Your identity is your foundation, shaping how you carry yourself, the choices you make, and the courage you embody. It is the bedrock upon which all achievements are built. Conversely, a lack of identity, a crisis in self-awareness, forms the foundation of failure and unhappiness. Without identity, even the greatest talents or the best resources will be misused or squandered. The tools are there, but without self-knowledge, they cannot serve their purpose.

Imagine a camera with a dirty lens; no matter how professional the camera may be, the images will always be blurry. Similarly, no matter how much potential or opportunity you have, if your understanding of self is clouded, your results will reflect that lack of clarity. It's not only about what you have, but how you see yourself in relation to it. Each of us has a natural inclination towards growth and fulfillment, but without clarity in our identity, we lose our way. A successful person isn't someone who's never failed or faced hardships; rather, they are someone who knew who they were and believed in their purpose, even when circumstances tried to lead them astray. As Henry Ford said, He who says he can, and he who says he can't, are both usually right. The difference lies in self-awareness.

Without a strong identity, even the most stunning buildings will crumble if built on a weak foundation. Discipline, goals, hard work, relationships, and even faith can carry you far, but without a solid understanding of who you truly are, it's all at risk. Many people climb their way to the top, only to realize their ladder was leaning against the wrong wall. They achieved everything except fulfillment, and their success feels hollow.

In my own journey, I've had moments of doubt, times when I questioned my own worth. I've held back from opportunities because, deep down, I hadn't yet acknowledged my true value. Whether shopping, booking travel, or making decisions, I often gravitated toward choices that felt safer or good enough. Looking back, I realize these choices reflected not my desires, but my fears and doubts. I completely believe I wasn't alone in this experience; many of us have held ourselves back, settling for less than we truly wanted or deserve simply because we didn't believe we were worthy of more.

The same is true in all areas of life. How often do we compromise in relationships, work, or life decisions simply because we are afraid of aiming for something more or better? If resources weren't a concern, how would you spend your days? What would you create? Where would you go? Who would you be or do?

This chapter isn't about encouraging reckless decisions but about challenging you to examine your beliefs about yourself. As Dr. Myles Munroe once said "When the purpose of a thing is unknown, abuse is inevitable." The purpose of your life, your work, and your time is something only you can define, but it starts with knowing who you are.

Time is passing, and with every day, you are writing the story of your life. Take time to reflect on the identity you portray daily, to question the path you're on, and to align your actions with your purpose. As you grow in self-knowledge, you'll find a new power—one that comes not from external success, but from an internal alignment with your authentic self. This is the journey toward a life that is not only successful but deeply fulfilling, driven by the power of knowing who you are and the purpose you're here to fulfill.

What drives you in life? This single question, deceptively simple, holds a depth that few ever truly explore. And yet, uncovering this answer is perhaps the most profound gift of love you can give yourself. In a world that constantly pulls us in every direction, it takes real courage to sit down and ask ourselves what, or who, is behind the wheel of our lives. What would your life look like if you took a moment to reflect, truly, on what's guiding you?

Like I stated it before now, Self-love is more than treating yourself with luxuries to comforts or conveniences and pleasures. Genuine self-love demands and begins with attention to your spirit, to the deeper needs that often go overlooked. It's the commitment to understanding your motivations, your guilt, your choices, and even your discomfort. Why do you make the decisions you do? Why do you choose the people who fill your life, the ambitions you pursue, the path you walk? Behind every decision is your identity—a battle each of us faces daily. At its core, this internal struggle shapes our choices, actions and, ultimately, our destinies.

One powerful insight from an anonymous philosopher claims that prolonged deprivation can imprint on the mind so deeply that even when the circumstances change, the mental impression remains. Think about this. Where in your life do you hold onto habits, programs or relationships because of an identity rooted in an outdated version of yourself? Every answer lies within you, ready to be uncovered. Let's turn to a surprising source of wisdom: **Isaac Newton's laws of motion.** I honestly admit, I wasn't the best science student during my school days. Physics, especially, was a big struggle for me. Yet Newton's insights have stuck with me since the day I was taught, resonating as metaphors for life.

The First Law states that without an external force, an object in motion stays in motion, and an object at rest stays at rest. How often do we continue on autopilot, sticking to routines simply because they're familiar? If we want to change our trajectory, we need and must apply an intentional force to bring about change.

The Second Law tells that the acceleration of an object is directly proportional to the force acting on it. The greater the force, the greater the impact. The same is true of our life goals, dreams and desires : with real intention and effort, our ability to change expands exponentially.

The Third Law reminds that for every action, there is an equal and opposite reaction. The energy you put out into the world is always met with a response. The question becomes, what kind of energy are you sending forth?

These aren't just physics principles—they're life principles. Each of us is influenced by forces outside our control, and yet our lives are shaped by the motivations within us. No matter our circumstances, no matter our beliefs or backgrounds, identity remains the fundamental driver that drives us. So the question becomes: **Who or what is behind the wheel of your life?**

The word drive comes from the Latin word- drivere, meaning to push, to steer, to lead. And that's exactly why we're here. Our time on Earth is limited—every breath counts down toward an inevitable end. Recognizing this reality can be uncomfortable, even frightening sometimes. But It's also liberating depending upon your identity. If you knew your time was finite, who would you choose to be driven by? I believe you will certainly employ a good driver who will not waste or play with it.

As humans, we're designed for purpose, just Like the incredible machines we've been gifted to create and invented. the electricity, planes, automobiles, the internet and ifinift others. through them our own lives have transformative potential. Just like these incredible machines and inventions, the beauty of their effectiveness depends on the identity of management. The same goes to our effectiveness as humans, our success, happiness, and fulfiments all depend on how well we're being driven. Too many of us coast, leaving our lives to chances and hopes, hoping someday things will change. Take a moment to see yourself becoming more intentional to take the wheel of your life, with purpose, with clarity and discipline. Remember: Time is quiet yet a faithful guide, Revealing all we carry within us. It shines on our strength, lifts us high and crowns our efforts in the sky. Yet time will turn, as time must do, Shifting paths, revealing truth. Those once praised by everyone may stand alone, and those once relegated may have everyones attention. Fame fades, power, not forever, praise will pass, Seasons change, as nothing lasts. Both in rise and fall, Our true identity remains. When we take charge of our time, we ultimately take charge of our lives.

CHAPTER 2

The big questions

Who? what? Why? And where? These are the biggest questions everyone literally has to answer correctly, in order to practically determine our life status quo and the direction we going

Who am i? What is driving my life? Why am I being driven? and where am I being driven to?

1. Who am I? Is a question of self identity, profile, and certainly the overall details that make up me.
2. What is driving me? this Is a question of passion, spirit and excitement, potential and gifts, and certainly the things that described your attitude and behaviors
3. Why am I being driven? Why am I here? This is a question of purpose and mission. the intention of your presence.
4. Where am I being driven? Is a question of destiny. your predetermination and expectations.

If you can honestly answer these four key life questions, you'll be able to remove the wrong driver that's been steering your life and let the right one take the wheel. These big questions are the foundation that form the characteristics of every life.

Life is a journey of learning, unlearning, and discovering. It's about growing from what's inside us and what we experience in the world around us. As long as our hearts keep beating and our lungs keep breathing, there will always be more to learn, more to see, and more to hear.

One big problem is that too many of us are often afraid to ask questions because we don't want to appear like they don't know something. But here's the truth—**not knowing something isn't truly the problem. Choosing to stay ignorant is.** Confucius once said, *The man who asks a question is a fool for a moment, but the man who doesn't ask is a fool for life.*

The worst kind of ignorance isn't just about facts—it's about not knowing **who you really are.** This is the most dangerous kind of blindness. A person who doesn't know themselves is bound to face struggles, confusion, and even lose out on their blessings. Imagine spending your whole life begging for things that were always meant to be yours and you never know about them.

How awful would it be to suffer and feel helpless, only to discover later that you were the answer to your own problems all along? All you needed was a change in mindset—from lack to abundance, from victim to leader, from human to divine.

Rumi once said, "*One of the wonders of the world is a soul sitting in jail with the key to its freedom in its hand.* This quote has always spoken deeply to me. Take a moment now—close your eyes and picture someone locked in a prison cell. He's scared, hungry, and hopeless, but the key to unlock the door is sitting right there in his hand.

Now think about your own life. Look at the struggles, the frustrations, the problems, and challenges holding you back. What if the solution has been in your hands all along? What if the only thing stopping you is that you haven't noticed it yet?

Many times, we're like that prisoner. We're searching for answers far and wide, running from place to place, hoping someone or something will save us. But the truth is, we're often looking in the wrong places. No matter how hard you search, you'll never find answers where they don't exist. This only leads to frustration and exhaustion.

To break free from this cycle, start by looking closer—closer to yourself. Ask questions. Make noise about what you need. Listen carefully to your own soul for guidance. Answers don't always come from outside; many times, they come from within.

Let me share a quick story to explain this.

A friend of mine once drove two hours to another city for some sort of engagements. When she got home, she couldn't find her house key. She thought she must have left it in the other city, so she drove another two hours back to look for it. Still, no key was found. In frustration, she called a locksmith. As she sat in her car, angry and tired, a small voice inside told her to check her bag one more time. She did—and there it was, hidden in a pocket she hadn't noticed before. Her frustration, the wasted time she has wasted and all efforts involved could have been saved or avoided if she had simply taken the time to look closer, listen to herself, and trust her instincts. This is how life works sometimes. We search far and wide for answers, running from one thing to another, only to find that the solution has been with us the entire time. If we pause, reflect, and trust ourselves, we can save so much time and avoid unnecessary suffery. So, let this be a reminder—your freedom, your answers, and your solutions may already be in your hands. You may simply need to stop, look, and listen to yourself. I was told a story some time ago about a man who was embarking on a journey to visit his old friend in another land. His ticket was purchased by his friend and sent to him, and it was a special business first-class ticket, which entitles him to all kinds of benefits and good treatments in the likes of drinks, foods. As he sat gently in the airplane as the journey proceeded, he began to see other people requesting and getting up to fill their glass with some top expensive labeled drinks and food of their choice. While he salivates, sniffing the alluring aroma from the food, and watching all the scenery throughout his journey, his thought was, I wish I could afford all these kinds of lifestyles as well like everyone here, but little did he know all he was wishing for were part of his paid ticket. only he could have taken the time to carefully read through his ticket, he could have possibly known his rights and entitlements. When he arrives at his destination, he begins to share his beautiful experience, and appreciating his friend for paying for his journey and also shares the experience of the kind of life he watched people lives in the same cabin with him in the airplane, and how he wanted to beg for a glass of white wine, but shame didn't let him do such. Then his friend was struck with the awe of his narratives, and asked him for his ticket, he brought it out and and he begins show him and listed out all that was supposed to be his entitlement in the journey, but his ignorance of self-identity makes him watch others live the same life he is entitled to, while he wishes. Our ignorance of who we are as an identity creates an express loop to becoming ignorance of what we have, then down to the things that belong to us, and this literally creates cloud confusion on the purpose of existence and ultimately takes many people to travel the wrong path in life and to finally end with wrong destination and unfulfillment.

It's our ultimate and primary responsibility, that We must know who we are, in order to know what rightly belongs to us, to know why we exist, what we should be doing, and where we should be ending up.

before you read further in this book, maybe, you are someone who has discovered who you truly are, what your drive is, why you exist, and where you are going with your life, or you are someone who still see yourself as someone who is still walking in a life clouded with confusion with no true knowledge of your true self identity, divine entitlements, drives and sense of direction. My goal in this book is not to lecture you about life in anyways at all, nor to offer myself as the wisest person who knows it all, but my prime purpose for this project is simple: my intention is to simply share my journey, personal experiences with you, what I have learned on my own way. Perhaps, there could be something that will serve as a blueprint to you in your own journey, either for the purpose of finding your way through, or to help you facilitate in your own route, or even maybe to simply to give you a thumbs up and smile to say good job on the path you have chosen. The truth is that we serve as light on the earth to lighten each other's path. the decision to make use of any proposition directed toward our lives is in our own choice to make like the legend Jim Rohn says, take advice not order. don't let anyone order your life. take what someone shares with you, think about it, ponder over it, and process it. take what you think is helpful and useful and discard what you think is not, without prejudice or guilt. Advice is something that can be freely given, the choice of what is useful is yours. Regardless of whatever currency you may have used, either in the form of money or relationships, to purchase this book, needless to say you must have to validate and accept everything I have written. my timeless advice is to kindly use whatever seems useful to you and discarded what don't without any form of prejudice

Here is one thing I have discovered in my own journey. regardless of age or location, It's absolutely okay to find yourself in a position not having knowledge of who you are at a certain point in your life. Knowing that you are not who you should be and where you Should be is the beginning of the journey to transforming your life. Every moment of an awakening is an opportunity to set up for a new trajectory. At least, that's how we all started to realize ourselves as human species on this earth. When you were first born into life, you obviously never really had any conscious knowledge about being human, nor have any knowledge of the environment that surrounds us, until we grew to a certain stage or years when our brains begins to develop to a certain stage and began helping in fixing meaning to things, and started interpreting the information of our sensories. That's how life is. Just in case you have been dealing with what I commonly call the identity crisis, or life entitlement crisis, or struggling to find happiness in life, I would like to tell you congratulations because you have picked up this book. By the end of our relationship together through your reading this book, you certainly will be able to vanquish all these questions that have brought so much unrest to your emotions and wellbeing.

There is no other reason why our lives can sometimes be invaded, and overshadowed with chaos, except for the reason for a missing puzzle in the box. We suffer emotionally and even sometimes physically as well, not for any other reason, but due to the lack of true knowledge. The lack of knowledge of who we truly are, the lack of knowledge of what is it in life for us, the lack of knowledge of why we are here, and finally, the lack of knowledge of where we are going. just as it is most profoundly written in Hosea 4:6 in the Bible. The people are destroyed simply because they lack knowledge. This is one fundamental pertinent portion of the scripture that most people never really think deeply to question further. Let's take for instance I am your school lecturer, at least just grant me this quick opportunity to claim this only for this moment: and I came to your lecture room to announce that every student will be subject to sort of consequences for a poor performers on a certain course, I believe any wise student that has faithfully been coming to classes and putting what seems to be his or her best will be certainly be poes to ask me further ask which of the classes is in reference are my talking about sir? Let's assume now you still have not asked yet. So let me do the asking still. In what areas is your ignorance? Perhaps you may have to take some time to come up with something in response, and that's absolutely okay. For instance if you don't have a financial surplus in your possession, you may say it is the lack of knowledge of money-making skills. What about those who have been married for a couple of years, They have done all they could and and all medical witnesses has confirmed them both good couples to have offspring together, but yet, they have not been able to hear the cry of a newborn baby in their homes, would you say it's because they don't know how to have close intimacy together? This is not to claim that most people that seem like having it going good are all good are perfectly equipped with how things work, but my take here is to let you know that sometimes things can still be stubborn even on the right track, and if you don't know yourself, you will certainly get off track. Sometimes, even at your own door with the right key, the locks can sometimes act strange and unusual, but you don't walk away from the door and throw the key away. There is an inner conviction that keeps you there by the door to ensure the door is opened and you are not giving in to the trick. Whenever you are being challenged or interrupted by a life test, the number one thing that has been required of you to vanquish whatever life challenges you with is not the badge on your shoulder, and the names we bear, but who we truly are. And anyone who has no knowledge of himself will either walk away from the right track to destiny, or keep in the wrong one., under the constant harassment of These life tests. Every test is a demand to show forth a virtue of what you already possess or claim.

Knowledge, at its core, is the revelation of truths that already exist. Imagine a beautiful sculpture hidden within a block of wood; the artist doesn't create beauty out of nothing—they reveal what was there all along. In life, the truths we uncover are like that hidden sculpture, waiting to be discovered, timeless and enduring. Yet, we often forget that true knowledge isn't just knowing facts or mastering skills; it's about uncovering our own true identity. Without this understanding, our lives can feel hollow, no matter how much we accomplish or accumulate.

When I first arrived in Denmark, I lived in constant fear. Every time I saw a police officer, whether in a car or on a bike, my heart would race. I was undocumented, and the identity card I carried—a leftover from a friend who'd left the country—was a thin shield against the law. I was impersonating someone else to get by: working, driving, even banking under a false name. Outwardly, I played the part well, but deep down, I know I was an impostor. Everything I accessed through that false identity lost its meaning because I knew it wasn't truly mine.

Over time, I learned that life is a series of missteps and corrections. Success isn't about avoiding mistakes; it's about transforming them into growth. Nearly every person who's achieved something significant has faced their share of setbacks—wrong turns in relationships, career missteps, financial pitfalls. Mistakes don't mean failure; the real failure is refusing to learn from them.

In fact, life itself follows a rhythm, just like a day divided into morning, noon, and night. How we start can deeply affect the journey ahead. Many people spend the early stages of life entangled in mistakes—wrong relationships, career struggles, business setbacks—mistaking these for permanent failures rather than lessons. We often convince ourselves we've found lasting love or the perfect job, only to be met with heartbreak or disillusionment. These disappointments push us to grow, to search again, and to redefine what happiness and success truly mean.

In today's world, many people have the wrong idea about success. Society tells us that money and influence are the ultimate goals, but this way of thinking often pushes aside what truly matters—things like integrity, kindness, and finding your purpose. When we were kids, we were taught to value honesty and humility. But as we grow older, the world pressures us to chase after wealth and status, sometimes at the expense of our values.

Let me be clear: money is important. It helps us take care of our families, stay healthy, and live comfortably. Even the Bible calls money a defense, meaning it's a valuable tool that can provide security. But here's the thing: money alone will never make your life meaningful. It can buy you a house, but it can't make it a home filled with love. It can pay for the most luxurious bed, but it won't give you peaceful sleep if your soul is restless. Money can surround you with things, but it cannot fill the emptiness inside.

Oftentimes, our desire to be rich feels like chasing butterflies. The harder we run after them, the farther they fly away. And in that desperate chase, we sometimes end up hurting ourselves, addicted to inappropriate despirations, damaging our health and body or even the people around us. But when we pause, relax, and admire life's beauty, the butterflies come to us and gently perch on our shoulders. This is a powerful truth about life: when you stop obsessing over wealth and instead focus on living with purpose and doing what's right, the blessings you're chasing often find their way to you.

This is what the Bible means when it says, Seek first the kingdom of God and His righteousness, and all these things will be added unto you. When you focus on living a life of integrity, kindness, and services, everything else—money, opportunities, fame, power, peace—will come in due time.

The secret to true success is not chasing after money; it's discovering your purpose and using your gifts to serve others. Each of us has something special to offer—a talent, a skill, or even just a kind word—and when we share these gifts with the world, blessings follow.

Here's another truth that many overlook: Give, and it shall be given to you. When you give freely—your time, your talents, your resources—you create space for even greater blessings to flow into your life. Think of a farmer: if he hoards his seeds out of fear, he'll never have a harvest. But when he scatters those seeds generously, the fields bloom with abundance. Life works the same way. The more you give, the more you receive—not just in money, but in joy, peace, and purpose.

The problem is, many people hold tightly to what they have, afraid that giving will leave them with less, they are not yet perfect enough to share their gifts, or what they have is not good enough to be shared. But the truth is, everything we've been given is meant to be shared. If you feel imperfect about sharing your gift, I suggest you embrace the beauty of making mistakes which I am going to share in the next chapter, and begin to share it imperfectly. And God wouldn't have put your gift in you if nobody would need it. you don't need to know who will need it, your first assignment is, that you just simply need to bring it to life. When you use what you have to make the world a better place, blessings come back to you in ways you never expected.

Look at the most successful people in the world. Many of them built their wealth by solving problems, helping others, or sharing their talents. They didn't just focus on taking; they focused on giving. And as they gave, the world rewarded them in return.

True happiness comes from fulfilling your purpose. It comes from living in alignment with who you are meant to be. In other words, happiness doesn't come from chasing simply material things. It comes from living with purpose and contributing to the greater good.

If you want true success, stop focusing on what you can get and start asking, What can I give? How can I use my talents to help others? What can I do to make life better for the people around me? What have I been through that I would like to help others to avoid? What did I see or admire somewhere that I would like to bring to my neighbourhood, community, state or even nation to change it for the better?

When you live with this mindset, money and other blessings will follow naturally. But more importantly, you'll experience a deep sense of joy, fulfillment, and peace.

Remember: success isn't measured by how much you take or hoard, but by how much you give. Money is a wonderful tool, but it's only one piece of the puzzle. The real treasure is living a life of purpose, sharing your gifts, love, and leaving the world better than you found it.

So, take a step back. Stop chasing. Focus on living with purpose and giving to others. You'll find that the blessings you've been running after will come to you when the time is right—just like those butterflies gently landing on your shoulder. True success is about living in harmony with who you're meant to be—and that is the ultimate richness anyone can attain.

CHAPTER 3

The Beauty of Making Mistakes

Mistakes often feel uncomfortable, even embarrassing, especially when we're trying to achieve something meaningful or new. But here's a profound truth I've come to embrace: mistakes are not failures unless we refuse to learn from them. Instead, they are stepping stones to growth, packed with lessons waiting to be discovered.

In fact, I've come to believe that I should make more mistakes—not recklessly, but boldly—because every mistake I've made so far has helped shape my life for the better. They've taught me humility, resilience, and adaptability, and through them, I've discovered strength I didn't know I had. A life spent making mistakes is not only more courageous but also richer in experience than a life spent playing it safe and avoiding risks. Whenever I hesitate out of fear of trying something new, I remember the words of Helen Keller:

Security is mostly a superstition. It does not exist in nature, nor do the children of men as a whole experience it. Avoiding danger is no safer in the long run than outright exposure. Life is either a daring adventure or nothing. I still remember when I started sharing my thoughts on social media, posting inspirational quotes and reflections on life. At first, I struggled. Turning raw ideas into clear, impactful messages felt overwhelming. My posts were riddled with typos, awkward sentences, and unclear thoughts. When I looked back at them later, I cringed with embarrassment.

I thought about giving up many times. Why should I keep trying when my work wasn't "good enough"? But deep inside, there was a spark I couldn't extinguish. Inspiration kept flowing, and I felt an unstoppable urge to share it.

Surprisingly, despite my doubts, people resonated with what I shared. I received messages from strangers thanking me for helping them find clarity or hope. Some even asked for mentorship, despite my own insecurities about my qualifications. That's when I learned a powerful truth: our imperfections don't disqualify us—they humanize us. People don't connect with perfection; they connect with authenticity.

Mistakes are part of the process. They teach us how to improve. If we wait to be perfect before starting, we'll wait forever. As Wendy Flynn beautifully said, Give yourself permission to be a beginner. The Bible shares an interesting parable in the story of Samson, where he says, Out of the eater comes something to eat, and out of the strong comes something sweet. This wisdom reminds us that even challenges, failures, and mistakes often bear unexpected rewards. What initially looks like a setback can turn into a blessing if we keep moving forward.

As I persisted in my writing, I stumbled upon writing tools like Grammarly and chatbots that helped me refine my writing craft. Over time, I became a better writer—not because I avoided mistakes but because I embraced them as opportunities to learn. Each stumble was like a sculptor's chisel, shaping me into a more skillful and confident communicator.

Mistakes aren't just obstacles; they're guides. They point out what doesn't work so we can discover what does. They reveal blind spots and encourage us to develop strengths we didn't know we needed. Every misstep is a lesson in humility, creativity, and perseverance. The real danger isn't making mistakes—it's letting regret paralyze us. Regret has a sneaky way of turning into a heavy burden pressing upon our strength, making us feel stuck and powerless. But here's a secret: regret only has power over us if we let it.

Taking ownership of our mistakes is a game-changer. Instead of dwelling on what went wrong, ask yourself, *What can I learn from this? How can I do better next time?* This shift in perspective transforms mistakes from being painful reminders of failure into opportunities for growth. Oprah Winfrey once shared this simple yet profound advice: that way through the challenge is to get still and ask yourself, what is the next right move? and then the next right move. and from that space the next right move. When you approach life this way, mistakes become stepping stones to wisdom, sharpen your judgment, deepen your character, and strengthen your resilience. Each time you rise after a fall, you grow closer to the person you're meant to be.

If mistakes are opportunities to grow, then the only truly dangerous mistake is refusing to step out of our comfort zones out of fear. Fear whispers lies: *What if I fail? What if I'm judged? What if I'm not good enough?* Fear is a smart enemy disguising as a friend. It acts as if it's protecting us, but rather robs us of every opportunity to showcase and become who we truly are. It keeps us from taking risks, from dreaming boldly, and ultimately from discovering our potential.

Regret, on the other hand, traps us in the past. It's like struggling against invisible chains that tighten with every negative thought. My grandmother shared a vivid metaphor for this: *Don't smash the clay pot to kill the rat hiding underneath.* In other words, don't let impulsive emotions like anger or regret destroy what is still precious in your life.

Mistakes are not the end of the world. In fact, they're reminders that we're alive, learning, and evolving. When approached with calmness and wisdom, even our mistakes can become stepping stones or springboard toward peace, growth, and understanding of who we are.

One of the greatest lessons mistakes have taught me is that true success isn't just about what you accomplish—it's about who you become. Without a clear sense of identity, even the biggest achievements can feel empty. I've seen people with wealth, fame, and influence still searching for happiness because they've lost touch with themselves. This often leads to destructive behaviours like addiction, narcistics behaviour, low self-esteem and insecurity.

T.S. Eliot once said, Half of the harm that is done in this world is due to people who want to feel important." But in reality, almost all harm—whether to oneself or others—comes from this deep need to feel valued. When people can't find self-worth from within, they try to get it from external sources, often in unhealthy ways.

The Bible uses two powerful metaphors to describe human beings: light and salt. Both elements are essential, and their impact cannot be overstated. When we fail to cultivate the qualities that make us inherently valuable, we look for substitutes—often in fleeting pleasures or destructive behaviours. As Viktor Frankl wisely observed, "When a person cannot find a deep sense of meaning, they distract themselves with pleasure." True fulfilment comes not from external validation but from an authentic connection to who we are meant to be.

Knowing who you are is a force that can withstand any storm. It gives you clarity in times of doubt and strength in moments of uncertainty. Mistakes don't threaten this identity—they deepen it. Each lesson you learn shapes your values, sharpens your vision, and reinforces your sense of purpose.

As George R.R. Martin wisely said, *Never forget what you are, for surely the world will not. Make it your strength, and it can never be your weakness.* Your mistakes are part of your story, not the end of it. They're proof that you're not your experience, you are growing, and striving toward something greater.

Wisdom comes from lived experience, and lived experience is rarely perfect. It's messy, unpredictable, and filled with detours. But that's the beauty of it. Every mistake you make adds a layer of depth and richness to your journey.

The key is to approach life with an open heart and a willingness to learn. Be patient with yourself. Give yourself grace when you fall short. Celebrate your small victories and the lessons hidden in your failures.

Remember, the greatest minds and the most successful people didn't achieve greatness by avoiding mistakes—they achieved it by embracing them. As Thomas Edison famously said when inventing the light bulb, *I have not failed ten thousand times. I've just found out ten thousand ways that won't work.* Mistakes are not roadblocks—they're milestones. Each one marks a moment of growth, a chance to try again, a step closer to your goals. Don't be afraid to take risks, to fail, or to stumble. Life isn't about being perfect; it's about being brave enough to keep moving forward.

So, embrace your imperfections. Trust that every mistake carries a lesson. With patience, faith, and determination, you'll find that even your setbacks can lead to sweet rewards. After all, life isn't a race to perfection—it's a journey of becoming.

CHAPTER 4

The Danger of Identity Crisis

H ere are the words of Lao Tzu I came across some time ago: He who knows others is wise; he who knows himself is enlightened. And as Brenda Shoshanna once said: Unless we base our sense of identity upon the truth of who we are, it is impossible to attain true happiness. A man lost in himself is like a ship adrift, without a compass or anchor. There is no better way to describe an identity crisis than through these wise words. An identity crisis is far more than a fleeting feeling of confusion—it is a deep, internal struggle that shakes the very foundation of who we are. It leaves one wandering through life without a clear sense of self, purpose, or direction. This state of uncertainty isn't just a personal issue; it affects mental health, relationships, the physical body, and even society at large.

Some time ago, I came across an article from Grand View Research discussing the remarkable growth of the cosmetic industry over the past few decades. The driving force behind this expansion? The relentless wave of advertisements bombarding consumers daily with the message that we are incomplete, flawed, and inadequate without their products. It's an outright war on our sense of identity, subtly yet powerfully shaping the way we see ourselves.

As I reflected on this, a vivid memory of a close friend came to mind. We had planned to attend an event together, but in the end, I went alone. The reason? The perfume she had ordered specifically for the occasion didn't arrive as promised. Despite having an impressive collection of high-end fragrances on her shelf, she had been so thoroughly convinced by one particular brand that she felt incomplete without it. She truly believed that without that scent, she wouldn't make the right impression or get her flower at the event.

That moment made me pause and think about how deeply we've allowed external things to dictate our confidence, our worth, and even our ability to show up in the world. Marketing thrives on one fundamental strategy—making us feel like we are dunce and not enough. The more we believe that our beauty, value, or desirability is tied to a particular product, the more we chase after things that were never meant to define us in the first place.

There's nothing wrong with enjoying nice things—whether it's a designer outfit, a signature fragrance, or the latest beauty trend. Luxury, style, associations and self-care can be beautiful forms of expression, but they should never replace the essence of who we are. A perfume can enhance your presence, but it should never dictate your confidence.

Makeup can highlight your beauty, but it should never make you feel unworthy without it. The things we own should complement us, not complete us. The place and people we associate with should be privileged to have your presence, and not you feeling nobody without them.

At the core of it all, we are who we are before what we have. Our worth is not measured by the brands we wear, the trends we follow, or the validation we seek from others. It is measured by the depth of our character, the kindness in our hearts, and the authenticity of our presence. Because at the end of the day, the most powerful thing you can wear is not a product—it's self-assurance, it's knowing that you are enough, with or without the extras.

True confidence isn't about what you wear, the brands you own, or the approval of others—it comes from within. It's rooted in knowing who you are beyond external labels and fleeting trends. But when we lose our grip on our authentic identity, we become vulnerable to outside influences. Society, peers, culture, and circumstances start shaping our choices, pulling us away from our true selves. The result? A life of disconnection, inner turmoil, and constant self-doubt.

I've seen this happen, not just around me but within myself at times. The moment we start questioning our worth based on external standards, we step onto a dangerous path—one that can lead to an identity crisis with far-reaching consequences.

One of the first signs of losing oneself is emotional instability. Without a clear sense of identity, emotions become unpredictable. One day, you feel confident and capable; the next, you're overwhelmed with insecurity. This emotional rollercoaster makes even simple decisions feel exhausting. I've felt this before—moments of deep uncertainty, anxiety creeping in because I wasn't sure where I truly belonged. A nagging sense of purposelessness. Frustration with myself, with others, with life's expectations. And if left unchecked, this chaos inside can spiral into hopelessness, making room for deeper struggles like anxiety and depression. When identity is unclear, decision-making becomes a nightmare. Instead of choosing from a place of purpose and self-awareness, we start making choices out of fear—fear of rejection, fear of failure, fear of being different. We go with the crowd, even when it doesn't feel right. We stay in situations that drain us, simply because they feel familiar. We silence our own dreams to follow the paths others have laid out for us. I've seen people settle for careers they hate because society tells them it's the smart choice. I've watched friends stay in toxic relationships because they feared being alone. And I've caught myself, more times than I'd like to admit, questioning whether my own desires were valid—simply because they didn't align with what was expected of me.

But here's the truth: the moment we stop letting the world define us is the moment we take back our power. We are not our possessions, our careers, or our relationships. We are not the standards imposed upon us. We are who we are— before anything we own, before any title we hold, before any validation we seek. Real confidence comes when we stand firm in that truth. The choices only deepen the disconnect between our actions and our authentic selves. Relationships require a stable sense of self to thrive. When someone is unsure of who they are, their interactions with others become strained. They might: Seek excessive validation, leading to dependency. Push people away out of fear of vulnerability. Struggle to set boundaries because they lack a clear understanding of their own needs. This instability often results in broken friendships, strained family ties, and romantic relationships that fail to endure. Ultimately, isolation sets in, compounding emotional distress. An unclear identity makes us more susceptible to manipulation. Without a solid foundation of self-awareness, we become easy targets for societal pressures, individuals with hidden agendas, or toxic environments.

As my godfather always says, There are only two kinds of animals in the jungle: the prey and the predator. When you are weak, every predator wants to prey on you.

This can lead to: Joining unhealthy groups or ideologies in an attempt to belong. Being exploited by others who take advantage of insecurity and ignorance. Conforming to trends or behaviors that feel wrong but seem necessary to gain acceptance. Over time, this vulnerability erodes trust in ourselves and others, leaving us feeling used and betrayed. Identity and purpose are deeply connected. Without a clear sense of who they are, individuals struggle to find meaning in life. This lack of purpose manifests as: Apathy and lack of motivation. Constantly jumping from one interest or career to another without satisfaction. Feeling trapped in a monotonous routine that offers no fulfillment. The loss of purpose leads to an existential void—where life feels like a series of meaningless tasks rather than a journey of growth and achievement. The psychological consequences of an identity crisis can be severe. Prolonged feelings of confusion, inadequacy, and despair contribute to chronic mental health struggles such as: **Severe depression**, where life loses its color and joy. **Anxiety disorders**, characterized by constant worry and fear. **Addictive behaviors**, as a means of escaping internal chaos.

Left unchecked, these challenges affect physical well-being, productivity, and overall quality of life. An identity crisis often leaves individuals stuck in a cycle of self-doubt and fear. They hesitate to take risks or make decisions because they lack confidence in their ability to choose wisely. This paralysis leads to stagnation, where life feels like it's standing still while the world moves on. It becomes a position where we are unable to move forward, backward, or even sideways. Stagnation becomes a breeding ground for regrets, filled with memories of wasted effort, time, and potential. The danger of an identity crisis is not limited to the individual—it ripples outward, impacting loved ones, communities, and society as a whole. A generation of people struggling with identity crises may: Prioritize superficial achievements over meaningful contributions. Experience higher rates of crime, desperation, and social fragmentation. Foster a culture of unwise comparison, where external validation overshadows authentic living. The result is a world where people are disconnected from themselves and each other, perpetuating cycles of confusion and dissatisfaction. Perhaps the most dangerous aspect of an identity crisis is its cyclical nature. The more a person struggles to define themselves, the deeper they sink into confusion. Each failed attempt to find clarity reinforces their self-doubt, making it harder to break free. This cycle can feel like quicksand—every effort to escape seems to pull them in further. Over time, this may lead individuals to resign themselves to a life of mediocrity, abandoning the pursuit of their true potential. A man cannot be comfortable without his own approval.– Mark Twain. The danger of an identity crisis lies not just in its immediate effects but in the long-term damage it causes to mental health, relationships, and a sense of purpose. It is a silent thief, robbing us of our potential and leaving us adrift in a sea of uncertainty. Recognizing the perils of an identity crisis is the first step toward understanding its profound impact on our lives. While the remedy lies beyond the scope of this chapter, one truth remains clear, and I sincerely want it to stick with you: remember, without a strong sense of true self, we risk losing everything that makes life meaningful.

CHAPTER 5

The power creativity

The entire purpose of writing this book is simple yet profound: to awaken you to the rare and extraordinary awareness of your truest nature. You might wonder, *What happens if I never write this book?* To me, the answer is clear: that would mean I've strayed far from my truest self. It would be a conscious choice to live under a false identity—a betrayal of self and the still, small voice within me that has persistently nudged me toward fulfilling this purpose. But this isn't just about me. It's about all of us. If you've ever ignored the quiet whisper inside—the one urging you toward a dream, a passion, or a higher calling—then you, too, have drifted from your authentic identity. This isn't merely procrastination; it's a loud and unmistakable sign that you're letting your life being driven by the wrong driver. Consider the heartbreak of parents in our society. They pour their love, effort, and sacrifices into raising their children, only to see those children grow into something entirely opposite to their hopes and dreams. It's not the rebellion itself that hurts most—it's the dissonance between what they believed they were shaping and what reality reveals. This gap often leads to depression, premature aging, and vulnerability to illnesses. It's not just about disappointment; it's about a deep existential disillusionment. When expectations of identity—both for ourselves and others—are shattered, the pain runs deeper than words. But here lies a sobering truth: just as parents suffer from misplaced expectations, so do we when we fail to live in alignment with our truest selves. The farther we stray, the greater the internal turmoil we endure. Within each of us exists two competing identities: one rooted in truth, the other in illusion. Just as we are composed of body and soul, light and shadow, so too are we constantly pulled between these opposing forces. A wise thinker once said, "Life is a constant struggle for territory. You are either being guided by who you truly are or by who you are not." Another likened life to a jungle, where you are either pursuing something meaningful or being pursued by fear, doubt, and distraction. The choice is ours: will we live as creators, or will we shrink into survival mode? The greatest tragedy of human existence is the fall from identity. When we lose touch with who we truly are, we drift into a life of reaction instead of intentional creation. We become like passengers in a car, watching helplessly as someone else takes the wheel. One of the smartest habits you can develop is to regularly evaluate the driver in your life's seat. Are you being led by your authentic self—rooted in creativity, purpose, and truth—or by fear, insecurity, and distraction? This question is not abstract; it's deeply practical. I once asked a friend how he'd feel if, while taking someone in need of urgent medical care to the hospital, the doctor on duty fled the room instead of treating the patient. At first, he laughed, thinking it was a joke. But when he reflected on the absurdity of such a situation, his response was profound: *That would mean the doctor is crazy, has no idea who he is or what he's supposed to do.* Exactly! When we shy away from our responsibilities, dreams, and challenges, we're like that doctor—forgetting the very essence of who we are. In Genesis 1:26, we're told that humanity was created in the image of God. Before man's creation, everything we know about God points to His creative nature. And even now, the beauty of creation reflects His divine essence. In the New Testament, Jesus reaffirms this truth in John 10:34, saying, Ye are gods. This profound statement is a reminder that we are not merely mortals stumbling through life—we are divine beings clothed in human form. And one of the most remarkable traits of God is His creativity. If we are made in His image, then creativity is not just something we do; it's who we are. To live passively, shrinking from challenges and opportunities, is to deny our identity. It's like the doctor who flees instead of diagnosing and healing. When faced with problems and challenges, do you initiate solutions, as the creator you are meant to be? Or do you retreat into fear, becoming part of the problem? The struggle to live authentically isn't a one-time battle—it's a lifelong journey. It requires courage, self-reflection, and a commitment to live in alignment with our highest values. Oftentimes, we are trapped in survival mode, driven by external pressures rather than internal truth. We chase societal definitions of success while ignoring the quiet voice within, whispering, *This isn't who you are. Here is the truth:* success in any endeavor hinges on this one thing: knowing yourself. When you anchor your actions in your truest identity, you unlock the clarity, resilience, and creativity needed to navigate life's challenges. So, let ponder over this when you encounter challenges, do you rise to the occasion as the creator you were designed to be? Or do you shrink back, allowing fear or doubt to drive your decisions? Remember, life is not about avoiding problems—it's about embracing them as opportunities to express your divine creativity. When you truly know who you are, every obstacle becomes a chance to create, to grow, and to leave your unique imprint on the world. Let this be your reminder: you are not a victim of life's circumstances. You are a creator, fashioned in the image of the ultimate Creator. Live boldly, authentically, and in alignment with your truest identity. Anything less is a disservice to yourself—and to the world waiting for the gifts only you can bring.

CHAPTER 6

Embracing Your True Identity

I still remember the evening my grandmother told me a story that changed how I see myself. We were sitting outside after dinner, under the warm glow of the setting sun. She looked at me with wise eyes, as if she could see my whole future, and said, "You are more than what the world tells you to be. Seeing my confusion, she began her story:

A hunter named Otono once found an eagle's egg lying alone in the forest. Not wanting to leave it, he took it home and placed it with the eggs his hen had laid. When the eggs hatched, the baby eagle grew up among the chicks. It acted just like them—pecking at the ground, running from danger, and flapping its wings only enough to lift itself a little. One day, the young eagle looked up and saw a powerful bird soaring high in the sky. Something about it felt familiar. It realized that, unlike the chickens, this bird belonged in the sky. A question stirred in its heart: Am I meant for more? The next morning, it saw the great bird again. This time, it didn't let fear stop it. It *stretched its wings not to flap like a chicken, but to fly. With one strong push, it lifted off the ground. The wind carried it higher and higher until it was no longer just watching the sky, it was a part of it. Grandmother looked at me and said, You were born to fly, not to crawl. The world may try to convince you that you're just another chicken, but never forget who you really are.*

I never forgot that story. And now, as I stand on the edge of my own journey, I ask myself: Am I still living like a chicken, or am I ready to spread my wings? One of the quickest ways to lose yourself is by trying to be like someone else. Each of us is unique, yet many people spend their lives hiding their true potential, never discovering their greatness. That is one of life's greatest tragedies. One of the fastest ways to lose yourself is by trying to imitate someone else. Each of us is born unique, a masterpiece of individuality. Yet, heartbreakingly, many of us spend our lives as imitations of others, suppressing our true potential, leaving our genius untapped and undiscovered. This is one of life's greatest tragedies.

From childhood, we are fed misleading ideas about who we are. These messages come from our environment, parents, schools, peers, and society at large. Over time, these external influences shape us more than our own inner truth. Even when the reality of our identity stares us in the face, we often resist it—feeling unworthy, afraid, or even guilty about embracing it. But why do we so readily accept falsehoods and reject the truth about ourselves? Because truth demands change. And change—though liberating—can feel terrifying and uncomfortable. No matter why people come to me—whether it's for business growth, career struggles, personal branding, relationship issues, or even just a general sense of confusion—our conversations always lead back to one thing: identity. Before we can fix anything external, we must first address what's happening internally. I once mentored a client who was struggling financially—barely able to make ends meet. As part of his growth journey, I gave him a list of affirmations to say daily:

I declare I am abundant, and abundance flows through me.

I declare I am enough, and enough flows through me.

I declare I am rich, and riches flow through me.

I am a creator, and solutions flow through me. When he first read the list, he hesitated. "Sir," he said, "*saying these things feels like lying to myself. If I were truly all these things, I wouldn't be struggling so much. How can I say something that clearly isn't true?* I understood his doubt because I had once felt the same. Years ago, when I was drowning in debt, struggling to pay rent, and barely able to support my children, I wrestled with the same thoughts. I wanted change, but I was stuck in the cycle of frustration—no matter how hard I tried, life kept pushing me back down. I explained to him, *These affirmations aren't lies. They are seeds.* Seeds don't grow overnight. You don't plant a seed today and expect a tree tomorrow. You have to water it, nurture it, and give it time. The Bible says, "*Let the weak say, 'I am strong.' Let the poor say, 'I am rich.'*" This isn't denial—it's a declaration. It's aligning your words with the truth of what you are capable of becoming. Most people believe that changing their reality starts with action. We've all heard it: *Take action! Work hard! Hustle!"* While action is crucial, it is not the first step. Imagine driving a car and deciding to change direction. Would you just twist the steering wheel without first deciding in your mind where you want to go? Of course not—that would be reckless. The same applies to life. Our identity functions on three planes of existence:

The Mental – What we believe about ourselves. The Spiritual – The energy and frequency we align with.

The Physical – The actions we take. For true transformation, all three must work together in harmony. If any of these are out of alignment, life feels like an uphill battle. When I was deadly strugglingly, literally with everything, both mentally, financially, relationship wise, socially and otherwise, I knew I was meant for more. I was hungry for growth, and I threw myself into taking action—seeking better jobs, building relationships, and I was aggressively looking for opportunities. But no matter how hard I worked, I found myself stuck. It felt as if life had placed a heavy stone on me, tying my hands and feet. Every time I got close to a breakthrough, new problems or expenses arose, keeping me at the same level—or worse. I remember a friend jokingly saying, *Your situation seems beyond ordinary.* He wasn't wrong. The more I tried to rise, the further I sank. I began to wonder if something unseen was holding me back—a curse, a cycle, an invisible force working against me. But then, everything changed when I aligned my spirit, mind, and actions. The Bible says in James

2:26, *Faith without works is dead.* But the reverse is also true: Action without faith and the right mental alignment leads to frustration. Your life changes when you shift your frequency. Energy cannot be created or destroyed—it can only be directed. When you tune into the right frequency, the right inspiration comes. And right inspiration leads to right action. No matter how hard you aggressively try and work to change your life, what I have learned in my experience is that until you begin creating our reality with the right frequency, you may never get what you want or seek. I have learned that things don't come, or happen to us, they come through us. Just as our children come through us, so does every other thing we desire. when aligned with the frequency of abundance, then abundance begins to flow through you. The same goes when we align with black and struggle, so also they become the dominant effect. So, I asked my client, *Do these affirmations reflect the life you want?* He thought for a moment and replied, *Yes, they do. Then,* I said, *keep saying them.* The transformation we seek isn't about becoming someone new—it's about returning to who we've always been beneath the layers of doubt, conditioning, and fear. Denzel Washington once said, *"True desire in the heart for anything good is God's proof to you, sent beforehand, to indicate that it's already yours.* If your heart deeply yearns for something, it's because it is already meant for you. Either you already have it within you, or you're on the path to acquiring it. The problem arises when we block ourselves with false beliefs and limiting identities. Transformation starts with words. Even if your mind isn't fully convinced yet, let your words pave the way. Just as thoughts can shape words, words can shape thoughts, and thoughts shape actions. In the beginning of creation, the Bible says, *"Let there be..."*—and everything we see today was spoken into existence. Never underestimate the power of spoken words. If you feel like you have nothing to start with, start with your words. Try this experiment: For 30 days, speak positive affirmations over your life—faithfully. If you do this with belief and consistency, unexpected doors will begin to open. The question isn't whether you can transform. The real question is: Are you ready to step into who you've always been?

Chapter 7

The Comparison Instinct

Don't compare yourself to anyone. We've all heard this advice, and at first, it sounds liberating. But in reality, it often leaves us feeling stuck or unsure. How can we exist in a world full of examples and expectations without comparing? The truth is, comparison is like a double-edged sword. Used poorly, it can steal our joy and fuel self-doubt. Used wisely, it can unlock our potential, help us grow, and cultivate gratitude.

Comparison is a natural part of human experience. It's how we learn. We recognize light because we've experienced darkness. We value warmth because we've felt cold. Similarly, we understand our strengths and weaknesses by observing others. The issue isn't comparison itself—it's how we compare. Do we use it to elevate ourselves or diminish others? Do we use it to inspire growth or cultivate self-criticism and resentment? My grandmother once told me a story about a young prince. His parents always reminded him, *"You are a future king, different from everyone else."* Instead of feeling special, he felt isolated and misunderstood. Seeking clarity, he disguised himself and lived among the villagers, hoping to discover what made him unique. At first, he imitated them, trying to blend in. But instead of feeling connected, he felt lost.

One day, he stumbled upon a broken mirror in the marketplace. As he gazed at his reflection, fragmented and scattered among the shards, he had a realization—his uniqueness wasn't about what he lacked or what he copied. It was about the qualities he could share with the world. This story illustrates that our individuality is like a fingerprint—unchangeable and uniquely ours. True self-worth isn't about conforming to external standards but about embracing and expressing who we truly are. Many people confuse individuality with personality. Personality is shaped by experiences, habits, and surroundings. It's how we behave, not who we are at our core. Individuality runs deeper—it's the essence of our being. When people lose touch with their individuality, they start valuing external markers like beauty, possessions, or achievements over internal growth. This often leads to envy, insecurity, and a fragile sense of self-worth.

Instead of comparing superficial traits, we can learn from the patience, courage, or simplicity of others. Some of the greatest lessons I've learned have come from observing the qualities that make others admirable. The poet Rumi once urged people to *"unfold their own myth."* Instead of borrowing stories from others, he believed in crafting one's own unique path. This type of comparison isn't about envy—it's about inspiration. Comparison can also be a gateway to gratitude. I once had a friend who cried after leaving her mother's house at the end of a visit. Her sadness was understandable, but I gently asked, *"Have you ever considered those who never knew their mothers or lost them too soon?"* This perspective didn't erase her sadness, but it helped her appreciate what she had.

During my divorce, comparison played a crucial role in my healing. Losing my marriage, home, and daily life with my children was devastating. I found myself sleeping in a hotel before a friend of mine, Ada, lent me her apartment to stay in, I was feeling as though my life had unraveled. One evening, as I sat in the parking lot overwhelmed by thoughts, I reminded myself that many in my position didn't even have a car to sleep in, let alone a hotel room. This perspective didn't diminish my pain, but it gave me strength and hope. Viktor Frankl once said, *"When we are no longer able to change a situation, we are challenged to change ourselves."* Comparison, when used wisely, reveals our resilience and the hidden blessings in life. Comparison can also remind us of our shared humanity. A friend once questioned my respect for Mufti Menk, an Islamic cleric. She asked, *Why would you listen to him? Aren't Muslims known for terrorism?* I responded, *If you were to be sick and the only doctor who could save your life was Muslim, would you refuse their help?* People should not be defined by their choices, not by labels. By comparing virtues—like kindness or wisdom—rather than stereotypes, we can foster understanding and personal growth. Nature offers a lesson in healthy comparison. Each season has its own beauty and purpose, yet they all coexist harmoniously. A tree doesn't envy a flower's bloom, and a river doesn't resent a mountain's height. Each plays a crucial role in the ecosystem. Similarly, when we compare ourselves to others, we should remember that we, too, are part of a larger design. Everyone has something unique to contribute. Life is like riding a bicycle—it's all about balance. Comparison driven by insecurity leads to jealousy and despair. But when rooted in gratitude and self-awareness, it fosters growth and resilience. Comparison isn't inherently good or bad—it's how we use it that matters. If it's driven by ego, it divides us. If guided by self-awareness, it connects, inspires, and helps us grow. The key isn't to eliminate comparison but to compare wisely.

When anchored in gratitude and individuality, comparison becomes a compass, pointing us toward our highest potential. It reminds us not of what we lack but of how blessed we are and what we can strive to become.

Every day presents a new opportunity. What will you do with it? Every blessing, even those disguised as struggles, holds value. Shakespeare once said, *"There is nothing either good or bad, but thinking makes it so."* Often, the most painful experiences become the greatest catalysts for growth over time.

Instead of allowing comparison to steal your joy, let it fuel your personal evolution. Learn from others, appreciate what you have, and strive to be the best version of yourself. After all, life isn't about being better than someone else—it's about being better than you were yesterday.

CHAPTER 8

Unlocking Life's Hidden Instructions

Your ultimate superpower lies in understanding the language of the universe. Too often, we push when we should pull, strike when we should speak, force what should be allowed, fight what should be surrendered to, and worry about what we should be grateful for. Life is always speaking and giving instructions at every given moment, the real challenge is our inability to learn and listen to understand life. If there is one reason why we often stumble into trouble, miss our purpose, or find ourselves overwhelmed by challenges that could have been avoided, it is our failure to heed life's instructions. Before danger strikes, before we make regrettable mistakes, and even before incredible opportunities and blessings come at us, the universe whispers to us—offering guidance through various means. These messages may come in the form of dreams, revelations, signs, symbols, coincidences, or even subtle gut feelings. Yet, more often than not, we ignore them.

Oprah Winfrey once said, *Life first whispers to you. If you ignore the whisper, sooner or later, you get a scream.* How many times have we looked back at a situation and realized that there were signs all along? There were things we could have done differently to better. That we had a feeling, a warning, or an intuition nudging us in the right direction, yet we dismissed it? Many people in toxic relationships, unfulfilling careers, or troubling situations admit that they sensed the red flags early on but chose to ignore them.

A few days ago, I was pulled over by the police and issued a ticket. Frustrated, I asked the officer why. He explained that I had ignored a traffic sign prohibiting a left turn. I protested, claiming I had never seen such a sign despite taking that route daily. The officer calmly advised me to check again. Later that day, I retraced my steps, and there it was—clear as day. The sign had been there all along. I simply hadn't been paying attention. That moment taught me an important lesson: instructions exist everywhere, guiding us toward safety, success, and fulfillment, but it is up to us to notice and follow them. Understanding and following the instructions meant to guide your life requires deep self-awareness and intentional action. There are key steps to unlocking these hidden instructions: your **Strength and Passion. Reason for Being. Self-Reflection and Intuition. Learning from Challenges and Pain. Action and Service.** The very first step is to recognize what energizes you. What is that one thing that sets your soul on fire, the thing that makes you lose track of time? It could be writing, speaking, creating, teaching, or building. Passion is the fuel of destiny, and your strengths are the tools you were given to fulfill your purpose. If you are unsure, look back at your childhood—before the noise of society clouded your vision. What did you love to do effortlessly? What brought you the greatest joy? These are clues to your life's instructions.

Beyond passion, ask yourself: *Why am I here?* Every individual is born with a purpose, a unique reason for existence. Your identity is not random—it was designed to serve a specific function in the grand tapestry of life. In Japanese culture, this concept is called **Ikigai**—the intersection of what you love, what you are good at, what the world needs, and what you can be rewarded for. Finding this alignment is key to unlocking life's hidden instructions.

Life's instructions often reveal themselves in moments of stillness. Our intuition—the inner voice that warns, guides, and reassures—is one of our greatest tools, yet we frequently override it with logic, fear, or societal expectations. Have you ever had a strong feeling about something, but ignored it, only to later regret it? That was your intuition speaking. Learning to listen to that inner wisdom through self-reflection, meditation, or journaling can help us tune into the instructions that are already within us.

Many of life's greatest lessons come wrapped in discomfort. Pain is often a teacher, revealing where we need to grow, what we need to change, and what we must let go of. The difference between those who succeed and those who remain stuck is how they interpret their struggles. Do you see your challenges as obstacles or opportunities? Every difficult experience carries a hidden instruction, guiding you toward transformation. Instead of asking, *Why is this happening to me?* ask, *What is this trying to teach me?*

Life does not reveal its full instructions to those who wait idly. Clarity comes through action. Sometimes, we delay decisions, waiting for a perfect sign from the universe. But the truth is, action itself is a form of discovery. Start where you are, with what you have, and the path will unfold as you move forward. As Rumi, the great poet, said, as you begin to walk the way, the way will appear. using your strengths to uplift others—is a powerful way to align with your true purpose. When you contribute to something beyond yourself, you begin to see the bigger picture of why you were created.

Not everything good is right for you. One of life's greatest tricks is placing us in comfortable but misaligned situations. Sometimes, we stay in jobs, relationships, or environments that feel *good enough*, but deep down, we know they are not where we are meant to be. The opposite of right is not wrong—it is often *good*. When you settle for "good," you risk missing out on "great."

To break free, you must first identify who you truly are, then align yourself with the instructions meant for your life. Every destiny has a blueprint, but you must be willing to follow it. The Bible reminds us: *"Ask, and it shall be given unto you; seek, and you shall find; knock, and it shall be opened unto you."* Whether you believe in God, the universe, or fate, the principle remains the same—there is an invisible source of abundance waiting to be unlocked. And the key? Your true identity.

If you feel stuck, lost, or unfulfilled, ask yourself: *Am I paying attention?* Have I been ignoring the instructions life has been trying to give me? Success, fulfillment, and happiness are not mysteries—they are simply the result of following the right instructions. Just as a road sign can prevent an accident, the instructions meant for your life can prevent unnecessary struggles and guide you toward your highest potential. Your destiny is already written. You don't need to create it—you simply need to walk it. Listen closely, follow the signs, and step boldly into the extraordinary life meant for you

CHAPTER 9

The path to Purpose and Fulfillment

O ne writer once said, *You can't hire someone to do your push-ups for you*. No matter how much you wish for it, someone else cannot build your muscles for you. The same principle applies to life—no one else can live your destiny for you. Many people wait for the world to tell them who they are, what they can do, and where they belong. But here's the truth: if you don't know yourself, the world will lie to your face. Society, circumstances, and even well-meaning individuals may define you based on their own limitations, expectations, or assumptions. But your identity is not something to be assigned—it is something to be *discovered*. Within you lies a force that fuels your soul with confidence, fulfillment, and joy. When you engage in something that aligns with your true self, you lose track of time and forget about external concerns like hunger, money, or even your surroundings. That state of being *in the flow*—completely absorbed and alive in what you do—is a key indicator of your identity.

For me, that experience comes through writing and speaking. When I immerse myself in these activities, I forget about time. My body fades into the background, and my soul takes center stage. What about you? Have you ever done something that made you feel fully alive, where your soul led the way, and your body simply followed? If so, that is a clue to your true calling. Many of us have lost touch with our true identity due to distractions, external pressures, and societal expectations. But one of the most effective ways to rediscover your purpose is to trace your life backward—to recall those moments when you felt most alive, most connected, and most fulfilled. These moments hold the blueprint to your destiny. Everyone faces obstacles that can obscure their path. Some get lost due to fear, doubt, or discouragement. But true success comes when you reconnect with who you were meant to be. This requires listening to the voice inside you—the one that knows what you are naturally good at, even if you feel unqualified or unsure. No one else can do what you were uniquely designed to do in the way that only you can. Just as no two fingerprints are identical, your life's identity is your personal, unrepeatable code. It is embedded within you and cannot be replicated by anyone else. The only person who can fully bring it to life is you. Many people fail to step into their true calling due to a few critical reasons: Failure to Discover Personal Identity – Not taking the time to understand who they really are. Indecision – Lacking the will to act upon their identity. Fear of Failure – Avoiding risks because of the possibility of falling short. Lack of Self-Belief – Doubting their ability to succeed.

This lack of self-knowledge and confidence prevents people from achieving their full potential. When you know who you are, optimism becomes your energy. Momentum carries you forward. Consistency keeps you on the path. Faith nourishes you. Focus becomes your guiding force, and determination leads your way. One of the greatest sources of confusion in life is the difference between pain and suffering. Pain is a temporary inconvenience, a necessary sacrifice encountered on the journey to success. It may be uncomfortable, but it eventually fades. Suffering, on the other hand, is the consequence of neglecting your true self. As Paulo Coelho wrote in *The Alchemist*: *Tell your heart that the fear of suffering is worse than the suffering itself. And that no heart has ever suffered when it goes in search of its dreams.* Pain is a sign that you are growing, evolving, and pushing toward your destiny. But suffering is the torment of never pursuing what you were meant to do. It is the slow decay of unrealized potential. Taking Responsibility for Your Life One of the biggest barriers to success is refusing to take responsibility. Many people blame their circumstances—government, family, finances, environment, or past experiences. But the truth is, we are not products of our circumstances; we are products of our responses to them. Life is 10% what happens to us and 90% how we respond to it. No excuse can justify not becoming the person you were meant to be. The only way forward is to take ownership of your identity and act upon it. Even when faced with challenges, an optimist sees opportunities where a pessimist sees only obstacles. As Winston Churchill said: *An optimist sees opportunity in every difficulty, while a pessimist sees difficulty in every opportunity.* Your challenges may be hidden opportunities—the very stepping stones leading you to your destiny. A few years ago, I needed to visit an office in Denmark for important information. I had the address, but no money for transportation. Even worse, I had overstayed my tourist visa and feared being stopped by the police. Hunger gnawed at my stomach, and uncertainty clouded my mind.

But I chose to walk—16 kilometers on foot, guided only by my phone's GPS. Along the way, I discovered parts of the city I had never seen before. I met a friend who, knowing my situation, generously gave me money for food. Eventually, I reached my destination, but the journey itself taught me an invaluable lesson:

When you take action despite your fears, life opens doors you never expected. Many people confuse money with success and happiness. But if money alone guaranteed happiness, why would the children of the rich still pursue education, careers, and passions? they could have just stayed back home having fun 24. The answer is simple: wealth without purpose is empty. Your true wealth is your identity—your unique talents, purpose, and contributions to the world. Some people are rich but unfulfilled because they are living false identities. Others may not have financial abundance but live with profound joy because they are walking in their true purpose. Your identity is not something to be given by society or external validation—it is something to be uncovered and lived. Until you stop making excuses and take responsibility for becoming the person you were destined to be, you will remain stuck in a life that does not fully belong to you. Les

Brown once said: *The best way to turn your life around is to cultivate an attitude of optimism, no matter how bad it gets.* As long as you are alive, your life will either expand or shrink in direct proportion to your courage. The question is, will you take ownership of your identity and live the life you were meant to live?

CHAPTER 10

Focus

Life has a purpose, and achieving that purpose depends on focus. Success isn't just about luck or talent; it's about committing to life's principles every single day. Failure, on the other hand, happens when we neglect those principles. It's not the big moments that define us but the small, consistent choices we make daily. As my grandmother always said: *The head that will not be defeated by obstacles will surely arrive at its destination.* Her words taught me a powerful truth: no matter how difficult the journey, staying focused is the key to reaching your goals. Sometimes life forces us to take a detour, but as long as we stay true to our purpose, we'll eventually get to where we're meant to be. But there's a deeper layer to this truth: focus isn't just a tool we use; it's an extension of who we are. This is why focus thrives in those who live identity-driven lives. When you know who you are, why you're here, and what you stand for, your focus gains clarity and purpose. The compass of identity makes focus not only easier but more powerful. At the heart of *The Identity Driven Life* is this belief: your true identity is the foundation of every decision, action, and direction in life. Being an identity-driven person transforms focus from a fleeting skill into a way of being. Focus is like a magnifying glass, concentrating the rays of your potential. Without a strong identity, those rays scatter, unable to ignite meaningful change. But when you know your identity—your core values, dreams, and unique purpose—you gain the ability to channel your energy effectively. Alexander Graham Bell said it well: *Concentrate all your thoughts upon the work at hand. The sun's rays do not burn until brought to a focus.* Identity gives focus a target. It aligns your actions with your values and helps you prioritize what truly matters. Without identity, focus flounders, jumping from one distraction to the next. But with identity, focus finds its center and direction. In today's fast-paced world, distractions are everywhere. Notifications, endless to-do lists, and the pressure to multitask all compete for our attention. But an identity-driven person has the advantage of clarity. They know what they're here to do and why, making it easier to tune out noise and focus on their mission. James Clear's words resonate deeply here: *Focus is the art of knowing what to ignore.* Identity-driven people can identify distractions for what they are: obstacles that pull them away from their purpose. This awareness allows them to protect their focus fiercely. Imagine two sailors navigating a stormy sea. One has a clear destination and a map; the other drifts aimlessly, blown by every gust of wind. The sailor with a destination—anchored in their identity—has the focus needed to stay the course, no matter how rough the waves. A few years ago, I was preparing to launch a YouTube channel, something I felt passionate about. I hired a freelancer to design the intro and outro. After several revisions, I still wasn't happy with the results, and frustration consumed me. One day, I was stuck in traffic, moving at a crawl. My phone buzzed with another notification from the freelancer. Without thinking, I picked up my phone to check the delivery. My mind wandered, consumed by thoughts of how to request a refund. In those few seconds, I lost focus on the road. Before I realized it, I had crashed into the back of a brand-new Audi A6. My car was totaled, and I didn't have insurance. That moment was a harsh wake-up call. It reminded me of Tony Robbins' wisdom: *Your life is controlled by what you focus on.* Looking back, I see that I had let a distraction hijack my focus because I wasn't grounded in the bigger picture of my identity. My purpose wasn't to argue over design tweaks—it was to create content that would inspire and help others. Had I been rooted in that awareness, I wouldn't have allowed a fleeting frustration to derail me. Identity acts as a filter for your focus. While I was sitting in that car having my hand behind the wheel, I was a driver-driving, and that calls for my full attention on the road. As my driving instructor will always say, drive when you are driving. The road deserves your full focus—anything less is a risk. When you're clear about who you are and what you stand for at every given moment, you naturally prioritize tasks and opportunities that align with your purpose. Consider this: when you know your identity, you no longer waste time chasing other people's dreams or trying to meet expectations that don't align with your values. You stop multitasking on things that don't matter and start single-tasking on the things that do. Steve Jobs captured this beautifully when he said: *Focus is about saying no.* Identity-driven people understand this better than anyone. They say no to distractions, fears, and doubts because they're deeply connected to their yes—the purpose that fuels their focus. Focus isn't just about discipline; it's about trust. When you trust your identity, you trust yourself to make the right choices. This trust allows you to be fully present, undistracted by the past or anxious about the future. Think about a tennis player returning a serve. They don't have time to dwell on a missed point or worry about the match outcome. Their focus is entirely on the ball at that moment. Similarly, an identity-driven person can focus entirely on the task at hand because they trust the bigger picture of their life's purpose. As Vince Lombardi said: *Success demands singleness of purpose.* This singleness of purpose is the hallmark of identity-driven life. It gives focus its true power: the ability to create extraordinary results by aligning your efforts with your purpose.

Here are a few practical steps to maintaining focus.

Define Your Identity Take time to reflect and meditate on your core values, passions, and goals. Write them down and register them in your mind. The clearer your identity, the stronger your focus will be. Set Priorities

Ask yourself: What truly matters to me? Use your identity as a guide to decide where to invest your time and energy. Eliminate Distractions

Create environments that support focus. Turn off notifications, set boundaries, and use tools like time-blocking to stay on track. Practice Mindfulness

Spend a few minutes each day centering yourself. Mindfulness helps you connect with your identity and stay present. Align Your Actions with Your Purpose. Before taking on a new task or commitment, ask: Does this align with who I am and where I'm going? If the answer is no, let it go. Focus, when rooted in identity, becomes more than a skill—it becomes your compass. It points you toward your goals, guides you through challenges, and keeps you grounded in your purpose. My grandmother's wisdom still rings true: *The head that will not be defeated by obstacles will surely arrive at its destination.* This journey isn't without challenges. Life will test your focus with distractions and doubts. But when you're anchored in your identity, you can navigate those tests with clarity and confidence. The power of focus lies not just in the ability to concentrate but in the ability to direct your attention toward what matters most. And what matters most is deeply tied to your identity. As Zig Ziglar said: *Lack of direction, not lack of time, is the problem. We all have twenty-four-hour days.* An identity-driven life ensures that your direction is clear, your focus is sharp, and your efforts are **meaningful. Choose to live from your true self, and let the power of focus transform your dreams into reality.**

CHAPTER 11

The Power of Optimism

L et's face it: life isn't easy. We all encounter challenges, setbacks, and moments when it feels like the world is against us. But here's the thing—how we react to those challenges defines our future. Will we rise above, or will we crumble under the weight? The answer lies in one powerful mindset: optimism.

Now, before you roll your eyes and think, *Optimism? Just thinking positively doesn't change reality,"* let me stop you right there. Optimism isn't about ignoring the hard stuff. It's about facing reality head-on but choosing to see possibilities instead of limitations. It's a shift in perspective, and believe me, it can change everything. Here's the deal: optimism doesn't magically erase problems, but it gives you the tools to deal with them better. Think about it—how many times have you faced a tough situation and thought, *I can't do this,* only to feel paralyzed? That's what negativity does. It robs you of the energy to act. Optimism, on the other hand, fuels action.

It's the voice in your head that says, *This is hard, but I'll find a way.* And when you believe there's a way forward, you start looking for solutions. Suddenly, what seemed impossible feels achievable. But let's be honest—staying positive when life is throwing punches isn't easy. It takes effort, especially when everything around you feels overwhelming. That's why optimism isn't just a feeling; it's a skill. And like any skill, it can be learned and strengthened.

When challenges arise, we all have a choice: do we face them as optimists or as pessimists? An optimist is hopeful and confident, no matter how bad things look. They see opportunities in obstacles, chances to grow even when things seem stacked against them. Optimism isn't about being naïve—it's about being resourceful and resilient. A pessimist, on the other hand, focuses on what's wrong. They get stuck in the problem, unable to see a way out. It's not that pessimists are bad people—they're just wired differently. But here's the good news: you can rewire your mindset. You can train yourself to think and act like an optimist. If you're wondering how to get started, don't worry. Optimism isn't some mystical power reserved for the lucky few. It's built on a foundation of small, intentional habits. Here are five keys to help you cultivate optimism and keep it alive even when life gets tough.

1. Know Who You Are Everything starts with knowing yourself. Who are you? What do you value? What are you capable of? When you're clear about your identity, you're less likely to be shaken by setbacks. Think of it like this: a tree with deep roots stands strong in a

storm. Your identity is your root system. The stronger it is, the more resilient you become. Many people miss opportunities simply because they don't believe they're capable. They see themselves as small, weak, or undeserving. But when you know your worth, you start approaching challenges with confidence.

2. Trust Your Source

Let me ask you something: where do you draw your strength from? Is it your faith, your family, your past experiences? Whatever it is, you need to trust and believe it fully. If you don't trust your source, the world is yours to explore. keep asking questions. questions shape answers, and answers shape destinies. Take Job from the Bible, for instance. He lost everything—his health, wealth, and family were stripped away. Even his closest loved ones told him to give up on his source for strength. But Job didn't lose hope in God. He said, *I know my redeemer lives.* His trust in his source gave him the strength to endure. When you anchor yourself to a reliable source—whether it's spiritual, emotional, or practical—you can weather any storm.

3. Learn from Experience

Your past is full of lessons. Every time you've faced a challenge and overcome it, you've built resilience. Those experiences are your secret weapons stored in your arsenal room waiting to be used.

Think about David when he faced Goliath. Everyone doubted him because he was young and inexperienced. But David didn't see himself that way. He remembered his victories over lions and bears as a shepherd and used those experiences to fuel his confidence.

The next time you face a challenge, take a moment to reflect on what you've already overcome in the past. It's proof that you're stronger than you think. your history of winning started even when you were yet unconscious of yourself.

4. Keep Your mind on the Goal

Let's be real—sometimes, life feels like an uphill battle. The only thing that keeps you going is the vision of what's waiting at the top. Whether it's a dream job, a happy family, or simply peace of mind, having a clear goal gives you purpose. It reminds you why you're pushing through the hard stuff. Think of an athlete running a marathon. The training is grueling, the pain is real, but they keep going because they're focused on crossing that finish line. We can do the same. Here's the truth: life will knock you down. It's not a matter of *if* but *when*. The question is, will you get back up? Resilience is about bouncing back. It's the ability to take a hit, learn from it, and keep moving forward. Optimism fuels resilience because it reminds you that failure isn't the end—it's just part of the journey. Let me tell you a story my grandmother used to share with me. It's about a tortoise who faced impossible odds but refused to give up. In a small village, the tortoise was falsely accused of crimes, as a way of conspiracy to deny him from being the next king of the community. He was convicted and sentenced to death. The elders conspired to throw him into a pot of boiling water. It seemed like the end for him. But instead of panicking, the tortoise did something strange—he started celebrating. His fellow inmates were baffled. *Why are you happy?* they asked. *you're about to die!* The tortoise replied, *Because I know this isn't the end. There's a throne waiting for me, and I won't stop until I claim it.* Here's the clever part: the tortoise knew so well that hot water would kill him—only cold water wouldn't. So when the elders threw him into the boiling pot, he starts to sings a cheeky song: *Hot water doesn't kill the tortoise, only cold water does! Like the saying goes, appear strong before your enemies even when you are weak.* The elders, feeling confused, frustrated and angry, decided to throw him into cold water instead. But the tortoise was ready. He pretended to die. one of the elders suggested the Tortoise should be buried, fortunately, another suggested it's better to rather just throw him out, allowing them to discard the Tortoise in the forest. Once free, he escaped and prepared for his coronation. When the day came for the gods to crown the next king, the tortoise was alive and well. His enemies were stunned as he claimed the throne they had tried to steal from him. What can we learn from the tortoise? Plenty. Never give up. Even when the odds are against you, there's always a way forward if you stay creative and resourceful.

Focus on the goal. The tortoise never lost sight of his crown, even in the face of death. Adapt to challenges. He turned a seemingly hopeless situation into an opportunity.

Most importantly, the tortoise teaches us that optimism isn't about avoiding problems—it's about facing them with creativity, preparation and courage. If there's one thing that can destroy optimism, it's self-doubt. When you stop believing in yourself, you start believing the negative voices around you. There's a saying I love: *He who sees himself as an ant should not complain when others step on him.* It's harsh but true. If you see yourself as small and insignificant, the world will treat you that way. Optimism starts with how you see yourself. Recognize your value, trust your abilities, and refuse to let setbacks define you. Optimism isn't a magic wand, but it works wonders. It gives you the strength to take risks, the resilience to bounce back, and the clarity to find solutions in chaos.

So, the next time life gets hard, remember this: since the beginning of time, challenges have always been disguised solutions waiting for the right mindset to convert them into opportunities. challenges are temporary, but your mindset lasts forever. Be like the tortoise. Be resourceful, resilient, and relentless. With optimism on your side, there's nothing you can't achieve.

CHAPTER 12

The Teacher Called Experience

Experience is life's greatest teacher. Every situation we go through—whether good or bad—has something to teach us. But here's the thing: we either learn from these moments and grow, or we let them pass by, wasted. The choice is always ours. Let me share one of my earliest lessons about experience, a moment that taught me how important it is to pay attention to life's teachings. When I was about three years old, life was simple. I lived in the village with my grandmother, surrounded by love and care. But the highlight of my little world was when my mother visited. She didn't come often, maybe once a year, but when she did, it was unforgettable. My mother was stunning, her presence can never be hidden. She would arrive with a warm smile and gifts, and her presence made everything feel different whenever she visited. One year, she brought bottles of liquid medicine and a lovely-smelling Vaseline for me. She gave me two teaspoons of the medicine every morning, noon, and evening, and oh, how I loved it! The medicine was sweet, almost like honey. If you've ever had those sugary multivitamin syrups as a child, you can imagine how much I enjoyed them. But one afternoon, my sweet tooth got the better of me. I decided I couldn't wait for my next dose. I sneaked into the room where the bottles were kept and reached for one. Without thinking, I gulped down the liquid. It wasn't sweet at all. It was bitter, horribly bitter. What I didn't realize was that I had picked the wrong bottle my mother never gave me before: chloroquine. I was allergic to it. Here is a lesson the hard way: Within minutes, my little body began to react. I started itching all over, and no matter how much I scratched, the itching wouldn't stop. It was unbearable! I cried and danced around, desperate for relief. My mother rushed to me, worried and confused. She tried to comfort me, rubbing my arms and scratching where I pointed, but nothing worked. Tears filled her eyes as she kept asking me what went wrong. Where have you been? Did you touch anything strange? she asked, her voice shaky with concern. But I was too scared to tell her the truth. What if she got angry? What if she punished me? So, I kept quiet, hoping the itching would go away on its own. It didn't. When my grandmother came back from the farm and saw the chaos, she immediately sprang into action. She tried everything she could think of—herbal baths, native chalk rubbed all over my body, and even chanting soothing words to calm me. But nothing worked. Finally, in her gentle, wise way, my grandmother coaxed the truth out of me. Eddy, she said softly, did you eat or drink anything you weren't supposed to? Through my tears, I confessed. I drank something from the bottle under the bed. My mother quickly checked the medicine bottles and found the one I had taken. Her heart sank—it was the chloroquine. She didn't waste a second. She grabbed me, and we rushed to the hospital on the back of a motorcycle. At the hospital, the doctor gave me an injection, and within minutes, the itching stopped. Relief washed over me like a cool breeze on a hot day. On the way home, my mother spoke to me in a calm but serious tone. Eddy, she said, whenever something is wrong, always speak up. Keeping quiet doesn't solve anything—it only makes things worse. If you had told me earlier, we could have helped you sooner. Her words stayed with me. That day, I learned that hiding the truth out of fear only prolongs our suffering. Sometimes, the consequences we fear aren't as bad as the suffering we put ourselves through by staying silent trying to avoid shame, and being punished. Experience taught me something valuable that day. It showed me that life is always teaching us, even in the smallest moments. The key is to pay attention and learn. Why Experience is Life's Best Teacher As I've grown older, I've realized that every experience— whether painful or joyful—has something to teach us. When we take the time to reflect on our experiences, we grow wiser and better equipped for the future. One of my favorite quotes from the philosopher Socrates is this: An unexamined life is not worth living. What he meant is that if we don't take the time to reflect and learn from what we go through, we miss the whole point of life. Think about it: when you make a mistake, do you take time to understand what went wrong so it can be avoided or amended? When you succeed, do you reflect on what you did right so you can repeat it, or upgrade on it? Every experience, big or small, holds lessons for us if we're willing to pay attention. Not all experiences are pleasant, but even the tough ones have value. Friedrich Nietzsche once said, That which does not kill us makes us stronger. Every challenge you face is an opportunity to grow stronger and wiser. Here's how you can make the most of your experiences: Reflect: After every major event in your life, ask yourself, *What did I learn?* Whether it was a mistake or a success, there's always something to take away. Be Honest with Yourself: Sometimes, the hardest part of learning from experience is admitting the truth to yourself. because honesty to oneself is the first step toward growth and change. Share Your Lessons: Don't keep what you've learned to yourself. Share your experiences with others—it might help them avoid the same mistakes or inspire them to keep going. Stay Open: Life's lessons don't always come in the form you expect. Be open to learning from every situation, even the ones that seem insignificant at first. The Power of Sharing Our Experiences In the confrontation between the stream and the rock, the stream always wins, not through strength but by perseverance. — H. Jackson Brown Jr. One of the most powerful ways to overcome life's struggles is by sharing your experiences with others. Your stories, no matter how simple or complex, can guide others through tough times and give them the strength to keep going. Sharing what you've been through creates a connection that helps others navigate their own challenges. Let me tell you a story about a musician who became very successful. He had once been a street hawker, selling plantains to survive. Instead of hiding his past, he turned it into a song called *Plantain Boy*. That song told his story of struggle and hope, and it became a massive hit. It didn't just change his life—it also inspired others to believe in themselves. His willingness to share his life opened the door to a future of abundance, for himself and the people around him.

This isn't just a one-time thing. All over the world, people who share their stories have found success and influence. In fact, sharing your life experiences can help others grow in ways that no school or university ever could. Why? Because stories are powerful. They inspire, teach, and heal. Whether you write a book, sing a song, give a speech, or create a video, your story can make a difference. Many of us believe the key to success is climbing the corporate ladder, working long hours, or getting fancy titles. But often, the key to freedom is already inside us—it's our own experiences. We don't see their value because they're not perfect. We think, *Who wants to hear about my mistakes?* But this is where we go wrong. Imperfect stories are the most powerful ones. Imagine if 80% of people who have faced failure—in their careers, relationships, or health—shared their experiences with others. They could bounce back stronger and even inspire the world around them. Unfortunately, fear of judgment often stops people from sharing. Instead of standing tall, they hide, missing the chance to help themselves and others. I know this because I've been there. At one point, I lost almost everything. My marriage ended, I lost my home and my business, my two cars were gone, and I was deep in debt. Worst of all, I lost custody of my three kids to my ex-wife. It felt like my life was falling apart. I remember thinking, *How can I motivate others when my own life is a mess?* I imagined what people would say: *You're not qualified to inspire anyone. You're a failure.* But then I thought, *What if I'm wrong? What if my story could actually help someone?* I decided to stop listening to that self-critical voice. If I had given in to shame and fear, this book wouldn't exist. Millions of people who need these words would have missed them. And here's something important I learned: the people who know about your mistakes are just a tiny fraction of the world. Most people don't know your past, and even if they do, they don't fully understand the journey you're on. It's not fair to let a few voices silence your story. There is beauty and power in imperfection. Your flaws make you human and relatable. Even if you didn't go to school or get formal training, life has taught you lessons that no classroom ever could. Your struggles have given you wisdom that is unique to you. These are the lessons others need to hear. Don't let fear or shyness stop you. Don't let the opinions of others hold you back. When you share your story, you heal yourself and give others permission to heal too. Your story can give them hope, courage, and direction. So, start now. Share your experiences. Write a book, sing a song, speak to a group, or start a blog. Use whatever tools you have, but don't keep your story locked inside. The world needs to hear it. And when you do, you'll be amazed at how many lives you change—including your own identity. My story about sneaking that bitter medicine may seem small, but it holds a powerful lesson about honesty, trust, and paying attention to consequences.

CHAPTER 13

Finding Light in the Shadows

The human spirit is stronger than anything that can happen to it.

—C.C. Scott

When I moved to Denmark, I thought my life would change for the better. I dreamed of a bright future, full of hope and new opportunities. But when I arrived, the reality was very different. It felt like walking through a dark maze, looking for a light that was never there.

I landed in Copenhagen with nothing but a suitcase of dreams and silent prayers. The city was cold, and everything felt strange. I spent my first days wandering the streets, trying to figure out how to survive. Just when I was about to give up, I got a call from Michael, a relative I hadn't seen in over 15 years. His younger brother, uncle Wilson had told him about my distress in the city of copenhagen. He invited me to Køge, where he lived with his wife, Esther, and their children. When I arrived at their home, I was welcomed with open arms. Their house was full of laughter and love, especially as they celebrated the arrival of their newborn son, Emmanuel. That evening, we had a barbecue in their backyard. For the first time in weeks, I felt like I belonged somewhere.

Michael was a pastor in Odense, a city that would soon shape my journey. He took me to his church and introduced me to a group of Africans who had built their lives in Denmark. They were engineers, nurses, students—people who had found success despite the challenges. I admired them but felt far from their reality. Michael let me stay in the church building in Odense. It wasn't a real home, but it was a place to sleep, and I was grateful. Life was still hard. I didn't have any legal documents, which meant I couldn't work or earn money. To survive, I began collecting bottles from garbage bins to recycle for a small amount of money. Early every morning, I walked through the streets, looking for bottles. The smell of the trash was awful, but hunger was worse. By 7:30 a.m, I would stand outside the supermarket, waiting to exchange the bottles for a few kroner. It wasn't much, but it was enough to buy some bread to eat in order to stay alive. Some days, even the little I managed to put together wasn't enough. One day, the burner in the church kitchen stopped working. I couldn't cook, and I had no money to buy food. I drank water to fill my stomach, but it only made me feel worse. That evening, as I lay on the cold floor of the church, my phone rang. It was Sister Martha, the mother of a church member. "Are you at the church?" she asked. Minutes later, she arrived with two large bowls of rice and tomato sauce. Her kindness left me speechless. She didn't stay long, but her help felt like a miracle. In that moment, I realized that even in my darkest times, I wasn't completely alone. I tried to make myself useful in the church. Every Sunday, I cleaned, set up chairs, and arranged instruments. Even though I had almost nothing, helping others gave me a sense of purpose. Without proper toiletries, I made do with what I had, a quick, dry bath and vegetable oil as lotion. One Sunday morning, as I was finishing up my work, a church member named Isabella arrived early. She greeted me with a big smile and said, Mufy, you look great today! Her words caught me off guard. I rushed to the bathroom to check myself in the mirror, thinking the vegetable oil had made my face too shiny. But when I looked, I saw someone who seemed better than I felt inside. Isabella's compliment stayed with me. For so long, I had seen myself as the poorest and most miserable person in the room. Her kind words reminded me that happiness isn't about what you have—it's about how you see yourself. Not every moment was about scavenging or church work. Sometimes, my friend Ikena and I went to bars that offered free beer during certain hours. It felt like a small break from the weight of my struggles. One night, I met a beautiful Danish woman named Sophie. We danced and talked, but her questions about my life made me feel exposed. Why are you in Denmark?" she asked. I didn't know how to answer. Our brief connection ended awkwardly when security guards interrupted us. Sophie left without saying goodbye, and I was reminded of how broken my life was. Days turned into months. Each day felt like a battle, but small acts of kindness kept me going. Sister Martha's meal, Isabella's compliment, and even small gifts from Esther reminded me that I wasn't forgotten. One Sunday, Isabella said something I'll never forget: Mufy, I know you don't have a job or a home, but you're the happiest person I've ever met. Her words made me think. I had been focusing so much on my struggles that I didn't see the small victories in my life. I wasn't just surviving—I was finding strength and even joy in the little things. The shadows in my life were dark, but they weren't all-consuming. There were moments of light—small, but enough to keep me going. I learned that my journey wasn't just about escaping the hard times. It was about finding hope and meaning, even in the middle of them. One day, I believed, I would step fully into the light. Until then, I would keep moving forward, one step at a time.

CHAPTER 14

Becoming

*What lies behind us and what lies before us are tiny matters
compared to what lies within us.*

-Ralph Waldo Emerson.

Murphy's Law is like a thief in the night—it strikes when you least expect it, indifferent to time or place. Just days after my heartfelt conversation with Uncle Michael, my phone rang again. Eddy, there's a problem," Uncle Michael said, his voice tense. My heart dropped. "What is it, sir?" I asked, bracing myself. The Odense kommune found out you're staying in the church building," he explained. "That wasn't part of my agreement with them. I've been risking it to help you, but now they're threatening to call the police if you don't leave. You have 24 hours to find another place to stay. The phone felt heavier in my hand as I lowered it. Where could I go? Who would help me now? The weight of those questions pressed on my chest like a boulder. I called Jolly, a guy I had recently met at church. We'd spoken briefly about my struggles, and he'd seemed understanding. But now, his phone wasn't connecting. I tried again and again, but there was no answer. Desperation grew. Next, I called Arnold, one of the youth ministers. I'm really sorry, Mufy," Arnold said after I explained my situation. "I wish I could help, but I'm not comfortable living with anyone. Even my own brother and I fight when we share space. But if you find a place to rent, I'll support you. But I don't have money, Arnold," I replied, my voice breaking. "I don't even know where to look for a place. Kelechi, another church member, crossed my mind, but he lived with his girlfriend. Everyone I turned to seemed to have their own reasons for saying no. I felt cornered, on the brink of losing everything. My greatest fear wasn't just being homeless; it was being the cause of further problems. What if the church's agreement with the kommune collapsed because of me? The thought of being responsible for their troubles made my stomach churn. As my thoughts spiraled, I stumbled across a YouTube video by Les Brown titled *Live Your Dream*. The title intrigued me, so I clicked on it. Les stood at a podium, speaking with a mix of conviction and warmth. At first, I thought he might be a pastor, but his message was different. He spoke about challenges, growth, and purpose. One phrase stopped me in my tracks: Adversity introduces a man to himself. I paused the video, letting the words sink in. Curious, I researched Les Brown's story. Born in an abandoned building, adopted, labeled "mentally retarded" in school—his life had been filled with challenges. Yet, he rose to become one of the most influential motivational speakers in the world. His journey sparked something in me. I remembered a moment from my childhood when my teacher had asked us to write about what we wanted to be when we grew up. While most of my classmates wrote they would like to become doctors or nurses, I had written: *I want to talk to and help people.* At the time, my teacher assumed I wanted to be a pastor or teacher. But even then, I had felt a calling—a pull toward something greater, though I didn't yet know what it was. As I reflected on these memories, my phone buzzed. It was Jolly. Mufy, where are you? he asked, his voice filled with urgency. Arnold told me about your situation. Don't worry—I'm coming to help you. Relief washed over me like a cool breeze on a hot day. Jolly arrived later that evening, his small student apartment in a university housing complex becoming my refuge. The room was tiny, barely big enough for one person, let alone two. But Jolly made it work. He offered me a bed and shared his meals with me. He didn't have much, but he gave what he could. His kindness reminded me that even in our darkest moments, there are people who shine their light for us. Living in Jolly's small room, I started to see life differently. I knew I couldn't rely on others forever. Every morning, I woke up early, walked the streets, and collected discarded bottles to exchange for a few coins. Despite the challenges, I found solace in my routines. I jogged through open fields, meditated, and reflected on my future. Slowly, I realized I wasn't just surviving anymore—I was becoming. One day, my younger brother James sent me a message asking for help with his school fees. I didn't have the money to support him, but I couldn't ignore his plea. When we spoke later, James admitted that his message was his way of getting my attention. He felt forgotten, and his words cut deep. That conversation shifted something in me. I had been so consumed by my struggles that I'd lost sight of my purpose. It wasn't just about surviving; it was about growing, evolving, and staying connected to the people who mattered. Les Brown's words continued to echo in my mind: Shoot for the moon. Even if you miss, you'll land among the stars.I was no longer defined by my hardships. Each challenge had shaped me, pushing me closer to becoming the person I was meant to be. The journey wasn't linear—it was filled with setbacks, small victories, and moments of clarity. Becoming isn't about having all the answers or reaching a specific destination. It's about the willingness to grow, adapt, and embrace every twist and turn. If you're reading this, remember: your struggles don't define you. What defines you is how you rise, how you grow, and how you use your experiences to shape your future. Surviving is just the beginning. Becoming is where the real magic happens. Keep moving forward. You are becoming.

CHAPTER 15

Despair

Sometimes when you're in a dark place you think you've been buried, but you've actually been planted.

— Christine Caine

L et me tell you something a little funny. Anyone who knew me back then would remember one thing for sure: my worn-out black sneakers. What they didn't know was that those sneakers had no soles. I was practically walking barefoot through the city. The fabric was torn and frayed, flapping with every step, but I held onto them. Not just as shoes, but as a symbol of stability an illusion I was clinging to.

Eventually, I couldn't hide it anymore. The soles were gone, and with them, my pride. I had no choice but to spend 120 Danish kroner—more than half of the 200kr I'd scraped together from returning bottles—on a new pair from H&M. To most, they were cheap, forgettable sneakers.

But to me, they were everything. They felt like a fresh start. They represented dignity. I wore them day and night, taking them off only when I laid down on the floor at Jolly's place. Later, I bought a few more pairs not because I needed them, but to remind myself of how far I'd come. They became quiet trophies of progress.

One Friday night, after drowning my frustrations in alcohol and loud music, I had a rare moment of lightness. I danced as though I had no burdens. But morning always brought a brutal return to reality. My head throbbed, the weight of my life crashed back in, and I staggered through the streets—no place to go, no energy for my usual jog. I ended up at the train station, pretending to wait for a train to Copenhagen, though I had no ticket, no destination, no plan.

I must've dozed off, because a gentle tap on my shoulder woke me. It was her. Let's call her Diana. She had captivated me for months—poised, radiant, effortlessly confident. She was on her way to school. Hours later, she passed by again, finding me in the same spot. Without saying a word, she walked into the 7-Eleven, bought a coffee, took a sip, and handed it to me. That warm cup felt like the kindest thing in the world. We hugged. She left.

I thought that would be the end of any chance with her. But life, it seems, isn't always so linear. Later, when things began to change for me, our paths crossed again—and for a brief moment, we had something real. Around that time, Uncle Michael became deeply worried about me. I had no job, no plan, no peace. He urged me to do a three-day dry fast and pray. I laughed bitterly. My life already felt like an endless fast—hunger and struggle were daily companions. But he was persistent. So was Jolly, who offered to fast with me for two days. That gesture broke through my pride, and I agreed.

Five days. No food, no distractions. Just raw reflection. The nights were long without clubs and alcohol, but deep down, I knew those distractions had never brought the change I was craving. When the fast ended, nothing changed outwardly, but something in me had shifted, I held onto hope a little tighter.

One fear haunted me most: the thought of becoming a father and failing to provide. I had felt the pain of growing up without a father, and I refused to pass that pain on. That fear shaped my relationships—especially with Emmanuelle. She longed for motherhood. At 30, she yearned for stability. But I wasn't ready. I couldn't bring a child into the storm I hadn't yet escaped. She called me emotionally unavailable, and she was right. I let her go without resistance. Love could wait. Survival couldn't. When I needed clarity, I often found it by the water or walking through the park. It was my sanctuary, a space to dream and reflect. One afternoon, the scent of grilled meat pulled me toward a group of young Africans, mostly Somali boys with Danish girlfriends. They welcomed me, and we hit it off. That night, they invited me out.

The club had always been my escape, and I joined them. But as we got closer, I discovered they were drug dealers. That truth hit me hard. I had vowed never to go down that road again, I'd seen where it led: lies, numbness, a detour from my purpose. Yet, I found myself smoking weed with them—not out of desire, but out of fear. I didn't want to offend them. I wasn't ready to face their judgment.

That night reminded me: when you leave something behind without replacing it, you risk falling back into it. Life abhors a vacuum. Like a jar that once held kerosene—empty it all you want, but unless you fill it with something new, the scent lingers. Temptation kept knocking. Help often came with strings, offers to return to that world. It made me question myself. Was this all I was good for? No documents. No job. No path. But I realized something else: where you search determines what you find. You won't find a car in a bicycle shop. Likewise, I wouldn't find purpose in nightclubs or in the company of dealers. I had to change my environment. So, I pulled away. It wasn't easy those nights numbed my pain. But I needed clarity. Eventually, the silence grew loud. My thoughts weighed heavier without the comfort of distraction. One day, in a moment of utter frustration, I told Jolly I was done. I was going back to Italy. Denmark felt like a dead end. Every step forward met with resistance. Jolly, God bless him, was tired too. He had done more than most would. But something deep inside whispered: Not yet. My prolonged stays at Jolly's place hadn't gone unnoticed. His flatmates started complaining, and one reported it to the dormitory janitor. This violated Jolly's housing contract, putting him at risk. I knew I couldn't keep staying there, but I had nowhere else to go. I thought I'd hit rock bottom with no job, no stability, just endless days of surviving. Then, out of nowhere, life threw me a lifeline. Joe Abaka, a friend I hadn't heard from in a while, called with a job offer at McDonald's. Four and a half hours each night. It wasn't glamorous, but it was something. And for the first time in a long while, I felt hope.

At first, things were looking up. I showed up on time, worked hard, and gave it my all. But then, life threw another curveball. Eric, a coworker, seemed to have it out for me. He went behind my back and told our manager, Mr. Williams, that I was unfit for the job. No warning, no discussion just like that, I was fired. I was crushed. Angry. Confused. I confronted Mr. Williams, demanding to know why, but all I got were vague excuses. The damage was done. That old, familiar weight crept back in the feeling that no matter how hard I tried, life was always there to pull the rug out from under me. But then, something incredible happened. My coworkers, Mads, Kristen, and Ali, stood up for me. They saw through Eric's lies and challenged my dismissal, even threatening to quit if I wasn't reinstated. Their support changed everything. Mr. Williams caved, not only giving me my job back but promoting me to a supervisor. Life has a funny way of working. A few weeks later, I found out Eric, the very person who'd tried to sabotage me, had lost his job and was struggling financially. Karma, right? But instead of feeling satisfaction, I felt something else. I saw myself in him, not the betrayal, not the deceit, but the desperation. I knew what it was like to be at rock bottom. So, I did the unthinkable: I went back to Mr. Williams and asked him to rehire Eric, under my supervision. Why? he asked, genuinely baffled. Why would you help someone who tried to destroy you? I smiled. "We don't repay evil with evil. An eye for an eye makes the whole world blind. Sometimes, kindness is the best way to teach a lesson. Mr. Williams hesitated, but eventually agreed. And when Eric returned, something had changed. The arrogance, the hostility, was gone. Maybe I was imagining it, but there was a humility in him that hadn't been there before. Over time, the tension faded, and in its place, mutual respect grew. Life has a way of softening people. Around this time, I reached out to Noble, a fellow church member, after hearing he had a room available. He was a student in Denmark, juggling his own struggles, but he agreed to let me stay for two weeks. The plan was simple: crash on his couch while desperately searching for my own place. Two weeks flew by, and I still had nowhere to go. I braced myself for the worst, but instead, Noble looked at me and said, "Stay as long as you need. Save your money, bro. You'll need it for bigger opportunities." That hit me deep. Here was someone who barely knew me, offering me something priceless: stability. For the first time in a long while, I could breathe.

As I reflected on my journey, I saw how much had changed, not just in my circumstances, but in me. Not long ago, I was begging for any job that would pay. Now, I was helping others land jobs. I introduced my friends, Victor and Kali, to opportunities, paying forward the kindness I had received. What struck me most wasn't the job, the promotion, or even the stability. It was the realization that my struggles were shaping me into the person I was meant to be.

Setbacks? They weren't punishments. They were lessons. And each one pushed me closer to understanding who I truly was. During quiet moments, I'd listen to mentors like Les Brown and John Assaraf, absorbing their wisdom. Success, I realized, wasn't about status or money. It was about purpose about discovering what sets your soul on fire and sharing it with the world.

Life keeps testing me, but something has changed. I'm not just surviving anymore. I'm growing. And that, more than anything, makes all the difference.

By January 2014, I returned to Italy to apply for a temporary permit to stay. I had submitted my extension application and waited anxiously for immigration authorities to respond. Days turned into weeks, and my financial resources began dwindling. I had sworn to never sell drugs again, and the thought of begging was out of the question. I also dont want to be a male escort anymore, it was neither sustainable nor ethical. As my situation grew more desperate, I felt trapped in limbo, unable to take meaningful action. My dream of living authentically seemed farther away than ever. I was slipping, betraying the clarity I held in my heart with inaction. One evening, a cousin to a friend of mine came by with a proposition that shattered my resolve. He needed someone to transport some grams of cocaine from Turino, a vibrant city in northern Italy known for its rich history to a city called Parma in northern Italy also known for its rich culinary tradition. My cousin, who knew my past well, had brought the offer to me. He expected a share of the profit, knowing I was out of cash and staying under his roof while awaiting my immigration decision. Against my better judgment, I accepted the job. As soon as I swallowed the drugs into my tommy, a sharp voice within me screamed, *You've failed yourself.* The momentary relief of receiving payment brought no joy— only a profound sense of confusion and self-loathing. I had compromised my integrity, and the weight of that decision was unbearable. In moments of desperation, I learned, we must tread carefully. The choices we make during such times can either uphold or unravel the essence of who we are. The money in my wallet only deepened my impatience with Italy. I felt an overwhelming urge to return to Denmark, where I had rediscovered purpose and hope. In Denmark, people around me aspired to be something greater, something meaningful. In Italy, it felt like the only aspiration was wealth. But returning to Denmark posed immense challenges. I was banned from entering Germany and Austria for 18 months, and Switzerland for 24 months—countries I needed to cross to reach Denmark without legal documents. Flying was out of the question until the Italian immigration authorities granted me legal status, and traveling by train was too risky with vigilant border patrols.

Desperately, I searched for alternative routes and stumbled upon a European car-sharing platform: carpooling.co.uk. Through this site, I found a Pakistani driver heading from Italy to Berlin. After contacting him, we arranged to meet in Verona—a city steeped in history, famously romanticized as the home of Romeo and Juliet. If I could make it to Berlin, my plan was to find my way to Hamburg, where my friend Julia had offered to drive me across the Danish border. It was a long shot, fraught with risks, but it was my only chance to escape the stagnation of my life in Italy. The driver's thick beard, reminiscent of Osama bin Laden, and his serious demeanor had initially set me on edge. His air of confidence was unnerving, but desperation forced me to trust him. He didn't know about my banishments or the risks he was unknowingly taking; if he had, he likely would have demanded an even higher fee. I paid the exorbitant amount he requested and boarded the car. Crossing the Austrian border without incident felt like a miracle. Each passing mile in German territory brought a small sense of relief, but it was fleeting. Just as I began to hope the journey would end smoothly, my worst fears materialized.

A sleek BMW overtook us just outside Munich, its passengers peering intently into our vehicle. I watched their expressions shift from curiosity to scrutiny, and my heart sank. Seconds later, the car slowed to match our pace, and the men inside signaled us to stop, flashing their batons. Police. I didn't need a prophet to foretell my fate. I had crossed this threshold before, and the outcome felt inevitable: arrest, detention, and judgment. My thoughts raced, desperately grasping at escape scenarios, but it was futile. The falsified documents I carried would only worsen my case, and my previous ban all but guaranteed jail time. The arrest was surreal, like reliving a nightmare. When we arrived at the station, my surroundings were unnervingly familiar—it was the same police station where I'd been detained a year earlier while trying to attend a wedding. The driver, now indicted for smuggling an illegal migrant, looked pale and furious. I, too, faced the stark reality of my actions. Stripped, searched, and locked in a cold, unwelcoming cell, I lay on a hard plastic mattress staring at the perforated window above me. The outside world was obscured, my freedom reduced to pressing an alarm for basic needs like water or a restroom visit.

My mind drifted to Wendy. The last time we spoke, I had let anger blind me. I'd said, "I hate you," in the heat of a fight.

Her stunned response still haunted me: *Mufy, do you really hate me?* I'd doubled down on the hurtful words, and now, I would have given anything to take them back. My heart ached with regret. I wanted to tell her the truth—that I didn't mean it, that my love for her was as steady as ever—but the cold walls around me rendered that impossible. On top of this emotional burden was the weight of my brother James' education. Wendy had helped pay his last school fees, and I had vowed to take responsibility for the next installment. Now, trapped and powerless, I could do nothing to fulfill that promise. Desperate, I begged the guards for a phone call and reached out to my cousin Vivian. "Please," I implored, "help me cover James' fees. I'll repay you as soon as I can." To my immense relief, Vivian agreed. A glimmer of hope broke through my despair—at least one promise could still be kept. But my incarceration remained a brutal reality. Days passed in limbo, each moment amplifying my regret. How had I ended up here again? My impatience, my impulsiveness, my broken promises—they had all led to this cell. If only I had listened to that inner voice, the one that had warned me in Verona not to take this journey. One evening, consumed by these thoughts, I closed my eyes and prayed. I prayed for forgiveness—not just for my actions, but for neglecting the still, small voice within me, the compass meant to guide me in times of crisis. I thanked God for the breath in my lungs, for the lessons hidden in my hardships, and for the possibility of redemption. A strange peace settled over me, fragile yet comforting, and I drifted into an uneasy sleep. A sharp knock at the cell door startled me awake. Through the small viewing hole, a guard called my name. I remained still, feigning sleep, but he unlocked the door and stepped inside. His gloved hands shook me gently, checking to see if I was alive. Startled, I opened my eyes. "I'm fine, I muttered. Annoyed, the guard stormed out, slamming the heavy door behind him.

Time dragged on. The tiny perforated window above provided little sense of day or night, and the oppressive stillness of the cell gnawed at my spirit. Finally, sleep overtook me again, and with it came a vivid dream. In the dream, my old friend Luvin appeared in the cell. There was no sound of the door unlocking; he was simply *there*. His presence was calm yet commanding, and his face radiated reassurance. Without speaking, he instructed me to remain tranquil, his words a balm to my frayed nerves. Before leaving, he delivered a message that felt heavy with importance: "When the judge asks for your opinion, tell him to let justice be tender according to the law." His tone was grave, his gaze piercing, as though he knew the weight of what he was saying. I woke abruptly, the dream lingering in my mind like a shadow. The cell was as cold and locked as before, yet something within me had shifted. Luvin's words echoed in my thoughts: *Let justice be tender according to the law*. I repeated the phrase to myself, committing it to memory. It felt like more than a dream—it was a directive, a lifeline from God guiding me toward what lay ahead. The next morning, the police arrived to escort me to the courtroom. As we approached, my heart pounded with a mixture of fear and anticipation. The words from my dream echoed in my mind: *Let justice be tender according to the law*. I clung to them like a lifeline, unsure of what lay ahead. Inside the courtroom, my interpreter greeted me, and I was directed to my seat at the defendant's table. The room was sterile and foreboding, its walls seemingly designed to drain hope. A lawyer moved about, preparing documents, while two officers stationed themselves near the entrance. Moments later, the judge entered. Everyone rose, and I stood nervously, studying his face. Was this the man who would receive the message from my dream? The proceedings began with the judge reading the charges against me. His voice was firm yet not unkind. "Do you admit to these offenses?" he asked. I nodded and quietly affirmed my guilt. He explained the penalties and outlined my right to appeal, though it was clear an appeal would be futile. I waited, my pulse quickening. Then, at last, he asked the question: "Do you have anything to say before sentencing? Summoning every ounce of courage, I recited the words that had come to me in the dream: *"Let justice be tender according to the law.* The room fell silent. The judge paused, leaning back in his chair as if weighing the significance of my plea. His expression softened, and for a moment, the tension in the room eased. Your words are unusual," he said, his tone contemplative. After what felt like an eternity, he delivered his verdict: six months in jail, with an option to pay a fine of 10 euros per day, totaling 1,800 euros. The amount was insurmountable for me, and the judge seemed to recognize my distress. He offered a reduction—5 euros per day—but even that was beyond my means.

Reviewing the police report, the judge noted the money found in my possession and proposed that the fine be paid from those funds. Relieved, I agreed and signed the necessary papers. The judge then pronounced my release, with one condition: I was to leave Germany and return to Italy. The police were visibly displeased with the judge's leniency. Back at the station, they brusquely handed me a seven-day permit to remain in Germany but refused to provide a ticket to Italy. Instead, they cited receipts for the meals I'd consumed in custody, using them as an excuse to withhold any leftover money. With no cash, a dead phone, and no one to turn to, I found myself stranded in the bustling streets of Munich. Despair clung to me like a shadow, but I refused to succumb. Wandering aimlessly, I stumbled upon a small train station and approached two black men for help. They offered little assistance beyond suggesting I head to Munich Central Station, where I might find others who could help. Grateful for even this meager advice, I joined them on a group ticket and made my way to the central hub. Munich Central Station teemed with life, a chaotic mix of hope and indifference. I approached countless strangers, asking for help, but was met with rejection after rejection. Just as my spirit began to wane, I encountered an older man from Malawi. His unkempt appearance and the scent of alcohol on his breath suggested a hard life, but his words carried wisdom. He spoke of his past as a once-successful drug lord, now reduced to homelessness. German police are ticklish," he warned with a knowing smile. His story was a sobering mirror of what my future could become if I didn't change course. As night fell, I found no shelter and curled up on a street corner, using my bag as a makeshift pillow. The cold seeped into my bones, and I prayed for another dream of Luvin to guide me. None came. At dawn, driven by sheer will, I resumed my search for assistance. By chance, I met someone who directed me to a non-governmental organization offering aid to migrants. To my astonishment, the building was the same one where I had spent the night outside in the cold, unaware of the refuge it offered. The organization welcomed me warmly, providing hot tea, food, and the luxury of a shower. After hearing my story, they arranged a train ticket back to Italy. As the train sped through the countryside, I reflected on the grueling journey. Every hardship had been a lesson. Ignorance, I realized, often magnifies suffering. Back in Italy, I checked the immigration website and discovered my application had been approved. I had been granted a one-year extension. The relief was overwhelming. Had I waited patiently, I could have avoided the ordeal in Germany entirely. Reaching out to Wendy, my girlfriend, I apologized for my anger and the hurtful words I had spoken before I left for germany. Her response was cold, a clear sign that she had moved on. Surprisingly, the pain I had anticipated didn't come. My mind was preoccupied with larger questions—questions about my identity and purpose. Despair tempted me to return to the streets, to the fast cash and fleeting comforts of my old life. But the image of the homeless man from Munich haunted me. He was a cautionary tale, a stark reminder of where that path led. I chose differently. The road ahead was uncertain, but I was determined to walk it with clarity, patience, and faith. Life's darkest nights often give way to the brightest mornings, and I was ready to embrace the dawn of a new version of my life.

CHAPTER 16

The Courage to Change

April 29, 2014. The cool, familiar air of Denmark hit me as I stepped off the train in Odense. It was a mix of emotions, coming back felt like returning home, but it wasn't that simple. I wasn't supposed to be here. My EU permit allowed me to stay for just three months, a small loophole that kept me from being sent away.

Whenever I ran into Danish police, the same question always came up. "When did you arrive in Denmark?" they'd ask. I'd reply, I just got here a few days ago." It was a safe answer, even if it wasn't completely true. Danish police were different from others I'd met—calm, polite, and never pushing too hard unless you gave them a reason. As long as you didn't cause trouble, they left you alone. But one wrong move could change everything. This stood in stark contrast to my experiences in Italy. There, the mere sight of a police car patrolling the streets could send a shiver down your spine as an african who is into street hustle. If you lived on the edge, hustling at night to survive, the last thing you wanted was for the police to notice you. If they did mark your face, they wouldn't stop you on the spot, but they'd remember your face. And the next morning, they could show up at your door, tearing apart whatever fragile sanctuary you had built.

In Italy, the streets were full of those who believed they could hustle their way to making money by selling drugs or peddling other illegal substances. But happiness? It always seemed just out of reach. Fear shadowed every move, and the sound of sirens in the distance felt like chains tightening around your soul. No amount of money could compensate for the constant anxiety, the shame, or the loss of dignity and pride. Life, as someone once said, is about balance, work and fun. If you work without a fun life, you're merely existing. If you only seek fun without contributing meaningfully, you're wasting away. In Denmark, I tried to find a rhythm that combined the two. The country's orderliness and strict supportive systems offered a sense of hope I hadn't felt elsewhere. The environment itself was both inspiring and challenging, pushing me to strive for something better.

A few days after my return, an old friend from Italy called. He asked, "Why are you moving back and forth?" To him, my travels between Italy and Denmark seemed aimless, like a man chasing shadows. I told him I was searching for something, but my answer didn't satisfy him. He assumed I'd return to Italy and resume hustling, but I had no intention of going back to that life. His disappointment was palpable, but I didn't care. Our paths had diverged long ago. He couldn't see it, but I had begun shedding the skin of my former self, the one that hustled in the streets, living day by day without purpose.

I deleted his number from my phone, not out of spite, but because I no longer saw us as aligned. Les Brown put it best: "Sometimes you have to ask yourself, what use is this friend? What energy are they bringing into your life?" This friend, whom I'll call Pato, represented everything I was trying to leave behind. We had sold drugs together on the streets, and during one of our conversations, I confided in him, "I need to find something better to do with my life." I thought he might understand or even support me. Instead, he laughed and told me to stay focused on the hustle.

"This is what our people have been doing for years," he said. They've made so much money doing it, and so will we.

That moment was a turning point. His words struck me as toxic, like an infectious virus threatening to derail my budding aspirations. I realized then that if I continued to keep company with people like Pato, I would never escape the cycle of survival. Growth demands separation, and I knew I had to distance myself before his mindset poisoned mine. Denmark offered me a fresh start, even if it wasn't without challenges.

My friend Kinsley was a beacon of stability during this time. He would visit every few weeks from Germany, where he lived with his wife, Petra. Whenever he came to Denmark, he would spend time with his son Elias, born to a Danish woman he had been with before meeting Petra. Kinsley's visits brought a sense of family and normalcy into my life. We would share meals, stories, and laughs, creating small moments of joy that reminded me what it meant to feel connected.

Despite my struggles, no steady job, no clear direction, I was beginning to believe that life didn't have to be a constant fight. It could be lived with purpose and grace.

My journey wasn't without moments of doubt and desperation. A contact from my friend Victor, whom I had once helped while working at McDonald's, led me to Mr. Jobe, a man infamous for his abrupt manner as much as for his success. Jobe was well-known in Odense, and though he had a reputation for being harsh, I saw him as someone who had found a way to thrive. He represented a reality I aspired to, freedom from the chains of mediocrity.

But Jobe also represented a choice. His rise had come at a cost, his approach to people was often dismissive and rude, especially when dealing with those without proper papers. I saw in him a reflection of the sacrifices and compromises people make when they prioritize success over kindness. I had to ask myself: What kind of success did I want? Did I want to rise at the expense of others, or did I want to build a life that inspired and uplifted those around me?

As I navigated these experiences, one question echoed in my mind: Why do you move back and forth? It wasn't just my friend from Italy who asked it, it was a question I asked myself. Was I searching for stability? For meaning? Or was I simply trying to escape the shadows of my past? Each step I took in Denmark brought me closer to an answer. I realized that my movement wasn't aimless; it was a journey toward self-discovery. I was shedding the chains of survival, redefining my identity, and striving to live a life aligned with my values. This is probably an opportunity for me to ask you the same question my dear friend asked me: Are you searching for purpose, or are you merely running from something? Remember, the direction of your movement matters more than its speed. Move with intention, and let each step bring you closer to the person you were meant to be. Life often places people in our paths who challenge our patience, test our identity, and push us to confront our realities. Jobe was one of those people for me. His words were sharp, his demeanor abrasive, and he seemed to revel in his power over others. Yet, for all his flaws, he was undeniably a hero to many. I couldn't overlook how he had helped countless individuals who had entered Denmark illegally find their footing, secure residency, and rebuild their lives. The dichotomy fascinated me: How could one man embody both salvation and scorn?

When I called Jobe asking for a cleaning job, I had braced myself for his curt response. He told me to call back in a few hours. When I did, his words were cutting: "Are you stupid?" He hung up before I could respond. My friend Kinsley, who overheard the exchange, burst into laughter—he had worked under Jobe before and knew his reputation well. But I didn't take Jobe's words to heart. Instead, I reflected on them. Perhaps if I had been living my truth—if I had embraced my identity as a writer and speaker—he wouldn't have dared speak to me that way. His harshness wasn't just a reflection of his personality; it was a reflection of my reality. I was asking for a cleaning job because I had strayed from the path of my dreams. Jobe's words, as bitter as they were, forced me to look inward.

His treatment took me back to a memory from 1997, during my secondary school days, a memory that had lingered in my mind for years. I often watched Mr. Okpere, our elderly school security guard. He was a man in his seventies, with a stooped frame and a gentle, weary smile. Despite his age and the wisdom it surely carried, he always responded to our young proprietor, Buddy, with an unwavering Yes, sir! Buddy, a man in his early forties, wasn't old enough to be Mr. Okpere's son, let alone his superior in life experience. It irritated me deeply to see an elder defer so much to a younger man.

At the time, I couldn't understand why Mr. Okpere didn't demand more respect. But as I grew older, I realized that life's circumstances often force us into positions of humility. Perhaps Mr. Okpere's life had been marked by missed opportunities or mistakes made in his youth. His Yes, sir wasn't just submission, it was survival.

In contrast, I thought of Rev. G.O. Oyakhilome, a man who had lived a life of purpose and fulfillment. Even in his seventies, he climbed the pulpit with the aid of a walking stick, his voice brimming with passion as he delivered his sermons. "I might seem retired," he often said, "but I'm only refined for the work I was called to do." His words were fire, igniting the hearts of those who listened. His frailty didn't diminish his power,it amplified it. He stood as a testament to what it means to live a life aligned with one's calling. These two men taught me a profound lesson: we all have a choice. We can drift through life, surrendering to circumstances like Mr. Okpere, or we can embrace our purpose and refine ourselves like Rev. Oyakhilome. The question is not whether we will face hardship,we will. The question is whether we will let it define us or refine us. At that time, I was far from living my purpose. Survival consumed me. Jobs were scarce, and I took what I could find. I ended up working on a farm owned by an Iraqi man, earning just 20 kroner an hour,a mere $3. For ten grueling hours a day, I labored in the fields, my hands blistered and my body weary. At night, exhaustion claimed me before I could even think about the motivational videos and biographies that once fueled my spirit.

I was trapped in a cycle of suffering. And deep down, I knew why: this was the penalty for abandoning my dreams. Writing and speaking weren't just aspirations, they were my identity. Yet here I was, buried under the weight of survival, unable to find a way out.

The questions haunted me: What should I write about? Where should I begin? Who would listen to me? Each question felt like a mountain, insurmountable and taunting. Yet I knew that avoiding them would only deepen my despair.

Determined to reclaim a sense of purpose, I set out to write an article for *The Copenhagen Post*, a bold exploration of how migrants and Danish citizens perceive Danish traditions.

I poured my heart into it, gathering a diverse group of friends for interviews: Jolly, a marketing student; Isabella, a nursing student; Ebenezer, an engineering student; and others from varied backgrounds. As I conducted these conversations, something stirred within me. Holding the small camcorder I had borrowed from the church, I wasn't just capturing their words, I was capturing my own rekindled passion. For the first time in a long while, I felt alive. But then, fear crept in. Kingsley, a friend, warned me against publishing the article. He spoke of others who had dared to critique the system, many had faced dire consequences: deportation, harassment, or worse. Denmark, a country I had grown to love, now seemed to demand my silence. Torn between my dreams and my survival, I chose the latter. I buried the article, silencing the voice I had fought so hard to rediscover.

This period of my life was defined not just by the physical grind of survival but by an internal war between fear and purpose. It was then that I thought of Melisa, a woman I had once considered building a life with. She was beautiful, vibrant, seemingly full of promise. But beneath her charm lurked a bitterness toward her child's father that unsettled me. Her anger, disguised as love, hinted at a darkness that could consume her, and anyone close to her. When I ended things, her smile turned cold, and I saw firsthand how quickly passion could morph into hatred. Her transformation was a lesson: to live inauthentically, whether in love or in life, is to invite bitterness. And I realized that if I didn't take control of my own path, I would meet the same fate. Life is a series of choices, each carrying its own cost. Jobe, Mr. Okpere, Rev.

Oyakhilome represented different facets of this truth. **Jobe** showed me the emptiness of power without empathy and kindness. **Mr. Okpere** revealed the consequences of drifting through life without the right direction. **Rev. Oyakhilome** embodied the beauty of purpose and fulfillment.

The question isn't whether life will be hard, it certainly will be. The real question is: will we use that hardship to rise, or will we let it bury us? I had two paths before me. I could continue surviving, or I could start *living*. Writing and speaking weren't just hobbies; they were my calling. And if I didn't embrace them now, I would pay the price of neglect later, perhaps even with interest. So I pose the same challenge to you: *Are you living your purpose, or are you merely surviving? Are you drifting through life, or are you refining yourself for the work you were meant to do?* Because the choices we make today will echo into eternity. With no immediate plans to fill up my days, I turned to motivational speakers, Eric Thomas, Les Brown, on youtube, absorbing their wisdom like oxygen to keep going. Their words weren't just inspiration; they were lifelines, guiding me out of the stagnation that had imprisoned me. But Diana, a woman I had once been drawn to, never understood. Whenever she visited, she would find me glued to my laptop, listening intently. She didn't ask why their words mattered to me, she didn't care. To her, these videos were distractions, an annoyance she had to endure when she was around. At first, I ignored her dismissiveness. But over time, her presence became suffocating. She mocked Les Brown's voice, exaggerated Eric Thomas's delivery, turning their words of power into jokes. She would grab my laptop, close it abruptly, toss it aside, and pull me toward her, demanding my attention in the only way she knew how.

And each time, I gave in.

The attraction between us had once been intoxicating. I had once thought I'd never win her over, especially after she found me sleeping at the train station and bought me coffee out of kindness. But now, I saw her for what she was, a distraction. Diana had no interest in what fueled me. Maybe, to her, I was only good for one thing. But at that point in my life, I needed *more* than just sex, I needed a companion who understood the fire inside me. Someone who wouldn't try to extinguish it. And so, I started pulling away. The desire I once had for her slowly turned to disgust. Then, there was Kristina, a woman who captivated me with her eccentric beauty. Her long, flowing hair, her striking figure, everything about her demanded attention. But she was wild. She burned through two packs of cigarettes a day, drank excessively, and lived as if there were no consequences. I tolerated her habits because I was infatuated with her presence. But deep down, I knew she was a detour, not a destination. Her lifestyle didn't align with my vision for the future. And in some ways, being with her made me feel like I was simply existing, floating through moments, disconnected from my deeper purpose. It was then that I understood something crucial: *The people we surround ourselves with either push us forward or hold us back.* I had spent too long sacrificing my dreams, dimming my light, and pretending that survival was enough. But it wasn't. I was done just existing. It was time to start living.

Tina, on the other hand, was the anchor of my survival. She was generous, passionate, and respectable, a woman in her late 30s who supported me through my toughest times. She provided for my basic needs, paying for my bills, groceries, and even my clothing. Yet, the age gap between us was a hurdle I couldn't ignore. When my birthday approached on September 18, 2014, I chose to celebrate it alone. Over a few bottles of Carlsberg, I reflected on my life and resolved to make significant changes as I stepped into a new year of my life.

The first decision I made was to end things with Tina. Despite her support, I knew we had no future together. She deserved more than I could give, and I wanted a relationship built on mutual dreams and aspirations. Letting Tina go was terrifying, I feared falling back into homelessness, as I had experienced before. But I took the risk after she had paid my October bills. I didn't have the courage to tell her directly. Instead, I made excuses to avoid meeting her. Eventually, Tina realized the shift in our relationship. By November, she suspected my intentions but waited for me to come asking for financial help, as I usually did.

By then, I had met Halldora, an Icelandic woman. We were still getting to know each other, engaging in conversations filled with curiosity. Kristina, being as unpredictable as ever, would show up unannounced, ringing my doorbell incessantly if I didn't answer her calls. Meanwhile, my financial troubles escalated. I was still jobless, and the housing company began issuing warning letters about unpaid bills. With a penalty of 400 kroner in the first week and 800 kroner by the second, they threatened eviction if I couldn't pay by the third week.

Desperate, I turned to Tina for help, but she laughed at my plight. "I thought you found your messiah to save you," she sneered, refusing to assist. No amount of charm or pleading could sway her. Fortunately, my friend Jolly came to my rescue, covering 80% of the amount. With my small savings, I managed to settle the bill. Yet, another round of payments loomed just days away.

I couldn't bear the thought of becoming homeless again, especially in Denmark, a country both brutally cold and expensive. Each day, I wandered the city in search of a job or someone willing to lend me money. Memories of sleeping in train stations and roaming the streets haunted me, amplifying my fears. The cold air, biting at my skin, seemed to mirror the coldness creeping into my heart. I feared that if I didn't change something, if I didn't take control of my destiny, I would once again find myself in the same grim position I had worked so hard to escape.

But even as I faced this overwhelming uncertainty, something inside me stirred. There was still a part of me that knew I wasn't meant to live this way forever. The struggle, though relentless, wasn't the end of my story, it was simply the beginning of a new chapter. The question remained: would I continue to survive, or would I take the leap and start living my purpose?

Eventually, I met Melisa, through a match on Badoo dating site. Victor, a friend, had uploaded my photo to his profile, and Melisa had been eager to contact me. We arranged to meet in the city, where we shared beers and exchanged stories. She showed me pictures of her adorable toddler and revealed that the boy's father had been deported from Denmark. When I asked how the father might reconnect with his son in the future, Melisa declared that she'd never allow him to ever connect with the boy. I asked her if he was dangerous to the child, he said no, but she claimed he was a serial cheater. Her adamant stance disturbed me. It wasn't the fact that she was a single mother, but her unwillingness to let her son know his father was an absolute turn off for me, being a victim of an upbringing without a father. she wasn't someone I could see myself with in the long term. One cool evening, Jolly came by and brought a few bottles of my favorite beer, Carlsberg. As we sat together, sipping and talking, we began brainstorming ideas about what we could do if the unthinkable happened—if the housing company made good on their looming threats. Our conversation was filled with both worry and hope, a mix of desperation and determination to find a solution. Suddenly, Jolly's phone rang. It was Arnold on the line. He wanted to know if Jolly was interested in taking up some jobs. Jolly, without hesitation, enthusiastically agreed to the offer. After ending the call, Jolly turned to me with a bright smile, his face glowing with a passion I hadn't seen in a while. I told you to relax," he said. "God never sleeps. He went on to explain that he'd go the next day to figure out the details of the job, but he was already planning to let me take it. While his optimism was encouraging, I couldn't shake off my lingering doubts. Even if the job worked out as he hoped, there was no guarantee it would save me from homelessness. After all, I wouldn't be paid until the end of the month, and my immediate troubles couldn't wait. The next day, Jolly called me again. This time, his tone lacked the usual excitement. "It's a very hard job," he admitted, "and I don't think you can do it. His words stung. Frustrated, I snapped, "What kind of hard job is it? It's a home demolition," Jolly replied hesitantly. Instead of feeling disheartened, I found myself smiling. "That's not hard at all," I said confidently. "In fact, it's the easiest job I could ask for right now, given my situation. The following morning, Jolly took me to the site. The house to be demolished was a six-bedroom, two-story building. He explained the tools and materials I would need for the job and introduced me to the homeowner, a man named Ali. The pay was set at 50 kroner per hour, roughly $7. It wasn't much, but it was a start.

I got to work immediately, tearing down the structure piece by piece. A few hours in, Ali arrived at the site. To my surprise, he began shouting at me angrily, ordering me to stop what I was doing. He threatened to call the police, accusing me of destroying his property without permission. Panic gripped me. He picked up his phone, appearing to dial a number, and I froze in fear. My heart raced, and my mind spun with thoughts of being arrested. Before I even realized it, I had wet myself out of sheer terror. I was on the verge of running away when Ali suddenly burst into laughter. It was all a prank," he said, his voice full of amusement. Ali approached me, patting me on the back as he continued to laugh. Relax, he said. I was just joking. Though my heart was still pounding, I managed a weak smile. That moment marked the beginning of an unlikely friendship between us. From then on, Ali treated me like family. He told his wife about me, and she began sending breakfast and lunch to the site every day. One day, Ali asked if I needed any money. It was as though he could see into my thoughts. Hesitating briefly, I admitted that I did. He handed me some cash, and I used it to pay off the overdue bills that had been keeping me awake at night. Despite the job's physical demands, the warmth and kindness from Ali and his family made it bearable. Slowly but surely, I dismantled the house, brick by brick, starting from the roof. My grandmother's old proverb came to mind: *It is one person who kills a dog in a village, but the entire community is labeled dog killers.* Ali was a living contradiction to the stereotypes I had formed about Arabs during my travels in Niger and Libya. As the demolition neared completion, I began to wonder what was next for me. The new construction phase required knowledge and skills I didn't have. My role was limited to destruction, and when it came time to build, I found myself left out. I realized then that I had been a tool, a weapon of destruction, and when the time for creation came, I had no place. Meanwhile, I worked to reconnect with my family back in Nigeria. My father had four children with my stepmother, all of whom were university graduates. There was Odianosen, a medical lab scientist; Wilfred, a civil engineer; Francesca, a pharmacist; and Isi, another medical lab scientist. All had been sponsored through school by my father, while I, the firstborn, had been abandoned to wander the streets as an outcast. But instead of dwelling on past hurts, I reached out to my siblings, rebuilding connections that had been lost. Introducing myself as their elder brother brought immense pride. Despite the years of separation, they welcomed me with open hearts, and our phone calls were filled with joy and laughter. One day, Jolly marveled at the relationship I had built with my father and stepmother. When I explained that this was the first time I'd truly connected with them in my 31 years of life, Jolly was shocked. Back at the demolition site, Ali often shared stories about his struggles as an immigrant in Denmark. He told me about living in a friend's basement with his wife, struggling to make ends meet. Over time, he saved enough to rent a shop, which doubled as a home. Today, he owns two homes and is building a third. His words were like fuel for my spirit. Things will get better," he often said. "Just keep going. Those words stuck with me. I began recording videos of myself at work, capturing moments of my labor as a reminder of the progress I was making. Months later, the demolition was complete. My time at Ali's house had ended, but our friendship remained strong. I knew I would carry the lessons I learned from him forever. The fire to become a writer and speaker burned brighter than ever. The journey ahead seemed daunting, but the dream remained alive. Somewhere, deep in my heart, I knew I would one day share my story with the world. Like the saying goes, silence is just the absence of sound, but a gateway to divinity. Sometimes, it's essential to give ourselves private, quiet moments—time to think and reflect. One day, I decided to switch off my phone and walk to a nearby park. Sitting alone, I let my mind wander, revisiting the twists and turns of my life. As I meditated, my thoughts drifted back to my early days in Nigeria, hustling for auditions to break into Nollywood. One man stood out during that time: Uncle Inegbedion. Though retired as an Assistant Deputy Superintendent of Police, he had a reputation for wisdom and directness. One day, he called me after a conversation with my father. "Have you ever thought about writing and acting in your own stories?" he asked. "You're an upcoming actor, why not create something uniquely yours? I laughed, dismissing it as a compliment I didn't yet deserve. "I'll think about it, sir, " I replied casually, but his words lingered. Sitting in that park years later, his suggestion returned with startling clarity. A voice within me said, *Begin with what you have: your life story.* But doubt crept in almost immediately, I had no idea how to write a book. Life had been a patchwork of struggles and triumphs, shadowed for years by a heavy burden of blame. I held my father and late mother responsible for the hardships of my upbringing, but reflection brought a profound transformation. Forgiveness became my freedom. I released the anger that had anchored me and embraced my stepmother and younger siblings with open arms, building stronger relationships in the process. At the same time, I committed to becoming a better, more accountable man, especially in my relationships with women. Kristina, a woman I once thought I loved, remained in my life. Despite moments of passion we share, I knew she wasn't part of my future. Halldora, on the other hand, had grown into a significant presence, and our relationship was becoming serious. Yet my own flaws threatened to undo it all. One evening, I stayed at Halldora's house. Before bed, I exchanged messages with Kristina on Facebook, sending a reckless and inappropriate message: *"When are you coming over to suck my dick?* Halldora joined me in the living room, and I hastily closed the tab on her computer, intending to log out later. But I forgot. The next morning, I left for work, unaware of the storm I'd unleashed. While at work with my friend Mike in the city, Halldora's message hit my phone like a thunderclap: *Don't bother writing or coming over anymore. I've seen your messages with Kristina. I'm done.* Her fury was justified, and I couldn't deny it. Embarrassed and defensive, I replied: *If that's what you want, fine. Trash my clothes that I have over at your place or burn them. Delete my number. I was never an angel before we met, and I can't change overnight.*

Her reply cut deeper: *Dirty ass.*

Though pride kept me from apologizing, her words lingered. That morning became a turning point. I ended things with Kristina for good and resolved to treat my relationship with Halldora with the seriousness it deserved. Halldora believed in me, even when I doubted myself. She noticed my growing interest in motivational speaking and writing, watching as I counseled people online. Messages of gratitude from strangers became my greatest joy. Inspired, I decided to post motivational videos to accompany my quotes. But fear held me hostage. I recorded several clips, only to delete them, silenced by self-doubt: *my English isn't good enough or Polish enough. I'm not like Les Brown or Tony Robbins. Who will listen to you, who will read your book?* Despite encouragement from those around me, the fear of imperfection paralyzed me. but funny enough I had no trouble mastering weddings and birthday parties as an MC. After every event I have hosted, people always come to me to tell me how much they love my energy, yet the idea of starting my journey as a speaker terrified me. I wanted to be flawless before I began. In a quiet moment, Halldora and I visited the city library to request books I'd always wanted to read: *The Alchemist, The*

Pursuit of Happyness, and *Live Your Dreams*. While waiting, I explored their stories online, finding inspiration in their journeys. A few weeks later, Halldora surprised me with a gift—she had ordered the books on Amazon and brought them to my house. I hadn't held or read a physical book in years, and the experience of reading those books was transformative. Chris Gardner's *The Pursuit of Happyness* resonated deeply. His journey from homelessness to Wall Street success sparked a fire within me. By the final chapter, I knew I had to write my own story. Jim Rohn's words became a mantra: *Your story is your power.*

At the time, I was working in a slaughterhouse in Gelsted, a small town in northwestern fyn in Denmark. My boss, Jobe, was known for his stern demeanor, but I didn't take it personally. Instead, I treated his harshness as a lesson in how *not* to treat others when working for you. Though Jobe assigned me just four hours of work daily, I always stayed for seven, ensuring every task was done to perfection. My dedication didn't go unnoticed. One day, the owner of the slaughterhouse, Per, a young man in his 30's, approached me to commend my work. Over time, Per and I developed a friendship. During one break, he shared how his passion for hunting became a thriving business. His story reminded me that true happiness comes from doing what you love. As the saying goes: *When you do more than you're paid to do, one day you'll be paid more than you do.* Jobe eventually increased my hours, acknowledging my efforts. Though it was a small gesture, it validated my belief in going the extra mile. Willie Jolley's words rang true: *When you do more than you're paid to do, one day you'll be paid more than you do.* Through work, reading, and reflection, my vision crystallized. My story was my foundation. I was ready to share it—not as a perfect speaker or writer, but as a work in progress. Life isn't about perfection; it's about growth. Every struggle, failure, and small victory has shaped my journey. Today, I embrace the imperfections that make me human and the lessons that push me forward. My dream is no longer a distant hope—it's a reality I'm building every day, one word, one story, one step at a time. After months of carrying emotional weight, life was finally starting to feel lighter. Halldora and I escaped to Malmö, Sweden, for a brief holiday, enjoying crisp air and quiet freedom in a cozy hotel. But that sense of peace was soon tested by an invitation: Halldora's aunt, Anna, was hosting a party at her office in Copenhagen. Though unsure how I'd fit in, I agreed to go, knowing it mattered to Halldora. The party was already lively when we arrived. The room buzzed with laughter and conversation as we greeted the crowd, the heat forcing me to shed my jacket and reveal a sleeveless T-shirt. We spotted Anna near the kitchen, her sharp eyes assessing us even as she smiled. After a warm welcome, she wasted no time getting to the point. What do you do for a living? she asked, her tone probing. Shame surged within me. I offered a well-rehearsed half-truth: "I'm a student at the University of Vienna." It was easier than admitting I was a cleaner, and I didn't feel worthy of calling myself a speaker or an author—not yet. Anna saw through my facade instantly. Her smile vanished, replaced by a cutting sneer. "You're nobody," she said, her words slicing through me. "A liar. Just a muscular black boy with nothing to offer but a long dick. You think you can fool my sister with that? Her words were a dagger, leaving me stunned. Halldora stood frozen, tears streaming down her face, too afraid to challenge Anna's bitter judgment. My chest tightened as I struggled to maintain my composure, responding to her cruelty with quiet humility. But inside, I was seething. As I turned to leave, Anna grabbed my shoulder. Her tone softened as she lit a cigarette. "I'm sorry," she said, her voice laced with vulnerability. She revealed that years ago, she had married a Ghanaian man, Kofi, who after gaining residency, he left her, and her life unraveled. It was a painful reminder of her past. Her story disarmed me. We smoked together, the tension easing as she apologized more sincerely. By the time we returned to the party, we were laughing, and Halldora looked relieved. But Anna's words lingered, forcing me to confront an uncomfortable truth: I was living without a clear identity. Back in Denmark, the weight of her accusations stayed with me. At a dinner with Halldora's friend, I faced the same dreaded question: What do you do for a living, Mufy? Once again, I lied, claiming my studies in Austria were on hold. That night, my conscience tormented me. How long could I keep deceiving others—and myself? The breaking point came during a Friday night outing at a bar in Odense. My friend Linux, an MBA student from Italy, had joined me. We sat with three accomplished women: two PhD students in medicine and a practicing dentist. When introductions began, Linux confidently handed out his business card, impressing the group. Then all eyes turned to me. What about you, Mufy?" one of them asked. Panic gripped me. For years, I had relied on lies, even pretending to be an actor—a ruse that always fell apart when people asked to see my work. Unable to answer, I faked a phone call and left the bar, walking home in tears. That walk changed my life. I made a decision: no more running from myself. I would confront the procrastination, excuses, and fear that had held me back. That night, I sat down to write, confronting every justification I had used to avoid my calling. Weeks of claiming I was too tired, months of telling myself I'd start later—it all ended there. In three months, I had written only 13 pages, a pathetic effort compared to what I knew I was capable of. But that night, I realized my story wasn't a source of shame—it was a mirror for others struggling to find their identity and their path, a guide through the storms of self-doubt. I committed to writing consistently, not just for myself but for anyone my story might inspire. Jim Rohn's words echoed in my mind: *Don't wish it were easier; wish you were better.* That night, I stopped wishing and started working. Anna's harsh words had planted a seed of transformation, forcing me to see the gaps in my life and the work needed to fill them. Now, every page I write brings me closer to the man I want to be—someone defined not by fear or lies, but by courage and purpose. If my story can help even one person find their own path, then every painful moment will have been worth it.

Chapter 17

The Power of Disagreement

Disagreement is often the catalyst that propels individuals, businesses, and nations toward transformative change. It's the birthplace of revolutions, where the discovery of one's true identity challenges the status quo. When we awaken to who we truly are, our first act is often to question and oppose the conditions that no longer serve us.

Too frequently, we endure unfavorable circumstances because our true identity remains dormant. A misaligned sense of self can lead us to accept subpar lifestyles and behaviors as normal. This isn't about lacking contentment; it's about being deprived of our fullest potential.

Ignoring this call doesn't just hinder our own growth and make us suffer; it drips losses to everyone connected to us. Conversely, embracing and acting upon our authentic identity not only enriches our lives but also uplifts those around us. As we liberate ourselves from our very one identity crises, our very presence encourages others to do the same. As Nelson Mandela once reflected, As we let our own light shine, we unconsciously give other people permission to do the same."

History and present experiences affirm this truth. An identity forged from profound disagreement fuels movements that persist until they realize their purpose. Life's challenges often erode our spirit gradually, making us complacent. Yet, reaching a point of deep dissatisfaction can ignite the fire within us to rise, challenge, and transform. As Thomas Paine observed, The harder the conflict, the more glorious the triumph.

Embrace the power of your true identity. Let it challenge the unacceptable, inspire change, and illuminate the path for others. In doing so, you not only reclaim your own destiny but also become a beacon of hope and transformation for the world around you. On December 1, 1955, a 42-year-old African American woman, Rosa Parks, was arrested for defying racial segregation on a public bus. She refused to give up her seat to a white passenger, as required by city law and societal norms—an act of quiet but firm resistance against an oppressive system that had long marginalized and dehumanized the Black community. Parks' single act of defiance ignited the Montgomery Bus Boycott, a pivotal moment in the Civil Rights Movement, led by the late Dr. Martin Luther King Jr. This boycott lasted 381 days that ultimately led to a Supreme Court ruling that declared segregation on public buses unconstitutional. Her courage became a powerful symbol of resistance against racial injustice, inspiring the ongoing fight for equality in the United States. That simple act of disagreement has not just shaped the lives of the living but also the ones that are yet to be born. There is this quote by Ralph Waldo Emerson that I find very fascinating every time it comes to mind. He says, To be yourself in a world that is constantly trying to make you something else is the greatest accomplishment. Like I wrote in the very first chapter of this book, time is a battlefield, not where we fight against time itself, but where we wages war againsts influences that does not aligned with our inner and authentic selves

Every revolution begins with a spark of disagreement. not always with others, but often with the version of ourselves we've been told to be. In 1930, India walked the walk that shook and crumbled an empire. Mahatma Gandhi didn't carry a sword or a flag. He simply walked. For 240 miles, barefoot on dusty roads, he marched to the sea to break a British law that forbade Indians from making salt, their own salt, from their own shores.

To the British Empire, it was a trivial matter. But to Gandhi and millions of Indians, it was everything. Salt became a symbol of self-respect. That walk was a disagreement with colonial identity created for Indians, a peaceful refusal to remain a subject of empire.

And with that disagreement, a revolution was born

There comes a time in life when we encounter situations that feel inherently wrong, unjust, misaligned, and undeserving.

These are moments that trigger an internal discomfort, a sense that things should be different. This feeling is not accidental; it is the voice of our identity calling for action and signaling that we do not belong in mediocrity, oppression, disrespect and limitations.

Disagreement is often perceived negatively, as an act of rebellion or resistance. However, in an identity-driven life, disagreement is a powerful tool—one that differentiates between those who accept circumstances as they are and those who demand better. When identity is strong and well-defined, it refuses to settle for situations that do not align with its essence.

At its core, identity is about self-awareness and alignment. It holds an internal compass that directs our values, purpose, and direction. When we find ourselves in situations that contradict our identity, an inner tension emerges. This tension, when harnessed correctly, is the catalyst for change. A certain man called Jabez was mentioned in first chronicle 9 in the bible. His mother named him Babez, meaning pain, because she bore him in sorrow or pain. One could imagine the diverstating coumpanding effect of such affirmation by everyone that knows him since he was born. Jabez rose to the awareness that his life don't have to be a reflection of the situation that surround how he was birth. Jabezs disagreement with the situation that surrounded his birth sparks his desire to pray. Like someone says, when life pushes you to your knees, you are in the right position to pray. Jabez prayed that God would bless him, expand his territory, protect him, and keep him from harm and pain, and God granted his prayers.

Disagreement is not merely rejecting an idea or circumstance; it is an active stance against undeserving realities. It is the refusal to conform to situations that diminish our worth, potential, or purpose. History is filled with individuals who changed their lives and the world by embracing the power of disagreement.

Think about figures like Nelson Mandela, who disagreed with apartheid, or Martin Luther King Jr., who disagreed with racial segregation. Their disagreement was not passive, it was a driving force that led them to action. Their identity refused to coexist with injustice, and as a result, change was inevitable.

In our personal lives, we must recognize the situations where our identity is in conflict with our circumstances. These could be toxic relationships, limiting beliefs, dead-end jobs, financial struggles, or unhealthy lifestyles. When you feel that discomfort, that sense of "this is not where I belong," it is your identity calling you to take action. The things we agree with in life- we accommodate, the ones we disagree with, it's our ultimate responsibility to influence, either by changing them or finding a way to live with them. Disagreement is a life steering wheel that we don't use often because life can be so sneaky that it does often pressure us enough to push the button. We agreed to every direction fate projects us until we ultimately hit disaster that often go beyond reviser and correction. But the good news is that with our identity we can change every undeserving situation. And the journey begins by recognizing misalignment: This the very first step towards a journey of transformation begins by identifying the areas of life where you feel discontent. What situations feel wrong? What areas of your life feel unworthy of your identity? Reflection and self-awareness help pinpoint these misalignments. own Your Right to Disagreement. don't feel stuck in undesirable situations believing you have no choice, you do have a choice. you have the power to disagree. You have the right to say, "This is not my story. I deserve better. Owning this right is the beginning of change. The event of the fire in the cane fields was an epic case of the profound power of disagreement. On a Caribbean island of saint-Donmingue, soaked in sugar and blood. enslaved Africans gathered in secret. For centuries, they had been told they were property to certain humans. That they had no souls. No rights. No worth.

But in 1791, they chose to gather in secret to unify their disagreement with these labels. Led by spiritual leaders like Dutty Boukman and strategic minds like Toussaint Louverture, they rose in rebellion, not just against the French plantation masters, but against the very idea that their identity was defined by chains.

They didn't just win freedom. They redefined it and became the first Black republic in the modern world.

Challenging Limiting Beliefs: Often, undeserving situations persist because of mental barriers. Thoughts like I can't change this or This is how things are, often keep us trapped.

And this is the biggest project of our Identity, changing these beliefs, replacing them with empowering truths. The identity we embodied tells our stories, the story we tell ourselves every day, about who we are and what we deserve. If your current situation does not reflect your desired identity, it's time to rewrite the script. Speak new truths: I am valuable. I am capable. I am meant for more. Taking Decisive Action: Disagreement is powerless without action. Once you recognize an undeserving situation, take the steps to change it. Whether it's leaving a toxic environment, pursuing new opportunities, or investing in personal growth, changing jobs or whatever it may be, taking the very steps no matter how small it be is a game changer. Like the saying goes, the only impossible journey is the one that will never begin.

While changing difficult can be daunting, Surrounding Yourself with the Right Influences can spark the beginning of miracles. Seek out people, mentors, or communities that reinforce your identity and encourage your growth and new tragetory. Disagreement with your current reality becomes easier when you are supported by those who see your potential rather than those who agree with who you are not. As a matter of fact, I believe that the best friends anyone will ever have are those who disagree with the wrong identity we carry. Change often comes with resistance. Society, family, or even your own fears and wrong identity you have embodied for a long time may push back against the decision to disagree with an undeserving situation. This is where resilience is necessary to stand firm in your identity and push through challenges by committing to lifelong growth. As you evolve, new situations will arise that challenge your identity. Keep refining, growing, and stepping into new levels of alignment.

To truly harness this power of disagreement, practical strategies are a necessity to turn discomfort into transformation. Here are key approaches to help you apply identity-driven change in your life:

1. The Identity Audit: List your core values, beliefs, and life goals. Compare them with your current reality. Identify where misalignments exist and decide what needs to change.

2. The Power of No: Learn to say no to situations that do not serve you. Reject and decide to walk away from relationships, opportunities, and habits that contradict your identity. Because every no to the wrong thing is a yes to the right thing.

3. The Vision Reframe: Envision the life you truly desire. Write down what your identity-aligned life looks like. While this may sound easy, the truth is that they are not also easy to. But if your happiness depends on it, then you must push yourself to act. Set clear, actionable goals to move toward that vision.

4. Daily Affirmations and Mental Conditioning: Reprogram your mind with affirmations that reinforce your identity. Use statements like I am, I declare, I deserve, whatever your new reality should be. Meditate on these truths daily to build confidence and clarity. Use your voice

5. Strategic Environment Shifting: Change your environment to reflect the life you desire.

This could mean decluttering toxic influences, changing social circles, changing cities, country, place of fellowships, or maybe simply upgrading your daily habits and behaviours. Your surroundings should inspire and reinforce your identity.

Living an identity-driven life requires the courage to disagree with anything that diminishes your worth, corrupts your content, suppresses your authenticity, potential, or purpose. It is about listening to the inner voice that is constantly nudging within, the saying, I am made for more, I deserve more than this, this is not where I should be, this is not what I should be doing, and acting accordingly to tuning this discord into a lifestyle where your inner being is proud with the way you live.

The power of disagreement is not about conflict—it is about clarity. It is about standing firm in who you are and refusing to settle for anything less than what aligns with your destiny. When you embrace this principle, you don't just change your life—you inspire others to rise as well. Disagreement is not the end of comfort; it is the beginning of transformation. Take the move. I dare you to disagree with unhappiness and unfulfilling life and step into the greatness your identity demands. Believe you can and Make the choice now.

CHAPTER 18

The Magic of Believing

There's a whole new level of power we unlock when we truly believe that what we seek is both available and possible.

I remember one time when I had to completely turn my living room upside down. I had just walked in from the parking lot, dropped onto the sofa, and settled in. A few minutes later, I got a call from my daughter's school. Sky was running a fever, and I needed to pick her up right away. I rushed to grab my keys, but... they were nowhere to be found. I had only walked from the parking lot to the living room, so logically, the keys had to be here. The car was locked—there was no way they could be anywhere else. After what felt like an eternity of searching, full of frustration and anxiety, I finally found them— dropped between the cushions of the sofa. What struck me was this: my search was focused entirely on the living room because I *believed* the keys could only be there, nowhere else. When you believe that what you want is available and possible to get, you are neurologically equipped to hussle and fight for it with a different level of power. That belief shaped my actions, even though I had no evidence to confirm that the keys were in the living room. This got me thinking about the stories of extraordinary people throughout history. The ones who defied the odds and changed the world. The ones who, despite repeated failures, kept pushing forward because they truly believed in their vision. Take Thomas Edison, for example—his belief in the light bulb invention kept him going through over a thousand failed attempts. Or J.K. Rowling, who had her Harry Potter manuscript rejected twelve times by publishers before it became one of the most successful book series ever. Or Tyler Perry, who invested everything he had into his first movie, *I Know I've Been Changed*, only to face failure after failure before he became one of the most influential filmmakers in Hollywood. We often don't dig deep enough into the insanity of their belief—their unwavering commitment to their vision. It's easy to quit when our first few songs don't chart, when our first book doesn't go viral, or when we don't build the lifestyle we imagined in the first few years of business. But if there's one thing I've learned from the stories of these great heroes, it's the authenticity behind their belief—the identity that drove them forward. Their belief wasn't just an idea; it was an unshakable part of who they were. That's what kept them going, even when the world told them it was impossible. It was their belief that set them apart, and it's the same belief we need to keep going on our own journeys. Belief is one of the most powerful forces in shaping identity, success, and fulfillment. What we believe about ourselves, our potential, and the world around us dictates our actions, decisions, and ultimately, our destiny. From history's great achievers to modern psychological research, the evidence is overwhelming: belief is the invisible architect of our lives. The way we perceive ourselves is largely a function of our beliefs. If we believe we are capable, intelligent, and worthy, we act in alignment with those beliefs. Conversely, if we carry limiting beliefs—such as I'm not smart or good enough or, I'm not meant for success or beautiful things—we subconsciously sabotage our own progress and put our power to sleep. Psychologists have long studied the concept of self-efficacy, a term coined by Albert Bandura. Self-efficacy refers to an individual's belief in their ability to succeed in specific situations. Bandura's research revealed that people with high self-efficacy are more likely to take initiative, persist through challenges, and ultimately achieve their goals, while those with low self-efficacy are more prone to give up. One of the most striking examples of belief shaping reality is the Pygmalion Effect, a psychological phenomenon where higher expectations lead to improved performance. In a famous study conducted by Robert Rosenthal and Lenore Jacobson, teachers were told that certain students in their class had extraordinary potential. Unbeknownst to the teachers, these students were randomly selected. By the end of the academic year, these students showed significantly higher academic performance. Why? Because the teachers' belief in their potential influenced their behavior, which in turn shaped the students' self-belief and performance.

This principle applies not just in classrooms but in every aspect of life. When we believe in ourselves, we naturally act in ways that make success and progress more likely. When we surround ourselves with people who believe in us, we thrive. Confidence is not something people are born with—it is built through belief. Consider the case of Thomas Edison, who conducted thousands of failed experiments before successfully inventing the light bulb. When asked about his failures, he famously said, "I have not failed. I've just found 10,000 ways that won't work." His belief in himself and his mission kept him going when most would have quit.

Similarly, Oprah Winfrey, one of the most successful media personalities in history, was fired from her first television job because she was deemed "unfit for TV." Had she accepted this belief, the world might never have known her impact. Instead, she chose to believe in her potential and used rejection as fuel for growth.

These examples show that belief fuels resilience. The more we believe in ourselves, the more we are willing to take risks, step out of our comfort zones, and persist in the face of adversity. While empowering beliefs can propel us forward, limiting beliefs act as invisible barriers to success. These beliefs often stem from childhood experiences, societal conditioning, or past failures. Some common limiting beliefs include:

I'm not good enough. Success is for other people, not me. I always fail when I try something new.

Neuroscientists have discovered that our brains are highly adaptable—a concept known as neuroplasticity. This means that with intentional effort, we can rewire our thought patterns and replace limiting beliefs with empowering ones. Here's how:

Identify Limiting Beliefs – Pay attention to recurring negative thoughts. Write them down and challenge their validity. Ask yourself, "Is this really true, or is it just something I've been telling myself? Replace with Empowering Beliefs – Once you identify a limiting belief, replace it with a more empowering one. Instead of "I'm not good at this, " say, "With effort and practice, I can improve. Use Affirmations – Positive affirmations can help reinforce new beliefs. Repeating statements like "I am capable," I am worthy," and "I am resilient" helps condition the mind for success. Surround Yourself with Believers – We absorb the beliefs of those around us. If you spend time with people who uplift and encourage you, your own beliefs will reflect that positivity. Visualize Success – Studies show that visualization activates the same neural pathways as actual performance. Elite athletes use visualization techniques to enhance their performance, and you can do the same to reinforce positive beliefs. History is filled with stories of individuals who changed the world because of their unwavering belief in something greater than themselves. Mahatma Gandhi believed in nonviolent resistance and led India to independence. Martin Luther King Jr. believed in the power of equality and inspired a movement that reshaped civil rights. Henry Ford believed that automobiles could be accessible to the masses and revolutionized industry with the assembly line.

One thing I have learnt is that none of these individuals had a roadmap or clearly saw the magnitude of the effect their effort could make when they started. What they had was belief—an unshakable conviction that what they envisioned was possible.

Start Small and Build Evidence – If you struggle to believe in yourself, start with small wins. Every success, no matter how minor, strengthens the foundation of belief. Reframe Failure as Learning – Instead of viewing failure as a dead end, see it as a stepping stone. Ask yourself, "What did I learn from this?" Every failure contains valuable lessons that shape future success. Adopt a Growth Mindset – Carol Dweck's research on the growth mindset shows that people who believe abilities can be developed through effort and learning achieve greater success than those with a fixed mindset. Practice Gratitude – Focusing on what you already have and what you've already accomplished strengthens positive beliefs about yourself and your life. Seek Role Models – Find individuals who have achieved what you aspire to. Study their journey, mindset, and the beliefs that propelled them forward.

Chapter 19

Never Give Up

Our greatest glory is not in never falling, but in rising every
time we fall.

– Confucius

Every time I feel like quitting something that means a
lot to me, I come back to this Earl Nightingale quote:
Never give up on a dream just because of the time it
will take to accomplish it. Either wisely or wastefully used,
time will pass anyway. It's like a little reminder from the
universe not to give up. It was the 26th of June, 2015, a Friday
a day that was supposed to mark a triumphant milestone
in my life. After months of relentless effort, sleepless
nights, and moments of self-doubt, I had finally completed
the manuscript for this book. I was ready to send it to the
publisher, but fate had other plans.

Three days earlier, on the 23rd, I had arrived at the library
before dawn. The sky was still dark, and the city seemed
to hold its breath. The library doors were locked, but I sat
outside, waiting, cradling my computer bag like it was a

treasure chest. It wasn't just a bag; it was the vessel carrying my dreams, my struggles, and every ounce of my resilience. When the library finally opened, I rushed in, claimed a table, and set up my computer. I connected the charger, plugged it into the wall socket, and watched as the screen began to glow. Excited to begin the final touches, I decided to use the restroom quickly while the computer booted up. I left my bag behind, feeling the kind of careless confidence that comes from focusing too much on the finish line and not enough on the hurdles still ahead. I was gone for less than three minutes. When I returned, my table was empty. My heart stopped. My computer was gone. The bag containing my backup drive— gone. My entire manuscript, months of work, endless hours of writing, revising, and dreaming—gone. I frantically searched the library. I approached the staff, desperate for answers, but they could only offer sympathetic shrugs. In that moment, it felt like the universe itself had turned its back on me. The weight of loss crushed me, and despair whispered in my ear: *It's over.* For hours, I sat paralyzed, staring at the empty space where my computer had been. Every sacrifice I had made to get to that moment played back in my mind like a cruel joke. The late nights, the skipped meals, the rejections and doubts—all of it now seemed meaningless. I began to question everything. What was the point? Why try at all when the world seemed so eager to snatch success away just as it was within reach? But in the midst of my despair, a different voice cut through the chaos. It wasn't loud, but it was firm, steady, and resolute. It said, *You have come too far to give up now.* I closed my eyes and let the voice grow louder. It reminded me of the purpose behind this book: to inspire, to heal, and to guide others toward their true identities. It wasn't just about me. It was about the lives that could be transformed by my story, the people who might find their own strength in my words. Quitting wasn't just a personal failure; it would be a betrayal of everyone who might one day read these pages and find hope. As I sat there, I remembered a motivational video by Big Brandon titled *Excuses Are Only for Bitches*. His words echoed in my mind like a battle cry: *Nobody cares about your excuses; they only care about your results*. Those words hit me like lightning. I realized I had a choice: I could let this setback define me, or I could rise above it and prove that resilience isn't just a concept—it's a way of life. The next day, I filed a report at the police station. The officer who took my statement seemed doubtful that I'd ever recover my belongings, but I didn't let that deter me. That same day, I returned to the library, sat at an empty table, and opened a blank document on a borrowed computer. Word by word, memory by memory, I began to reconstruct my manuscript. I didn't focus on how much I had lost; I focused on how much I still had to give. Each sentence was a declaration of defiance, each paragraph a testament to perseverance. The process was slow and painful, but with every keystroke, I felt the fire inside me burned brighter. Through this ordeal, I learned that life's greatest triumphs are often born from its deepest struggles. Pain, I realized, is not a dead end—it's the raw material required to build success. And success isn't about what you achieve; it's about who you become in the process. Today, as you finish this book, you hold in your hands not just a collection of words but a piece of my soul. This book is proof that no matter how many times you fall, what truly matters is that you get back up. it's a reminder that a setback is not a knockout, rather its a set up for a better come back. It's a reminder that the hero you seek is already within you, waiting for you to believe. I don't have all the riches in the world, and I don't wish for them. What I have is far more valuable: clarity of purpose, unshakable resilience, and the deep love of my family. Above all, I have found my identity—the core of who I am and the reason I exist. This is what allows me to live my dream and find joy in the simple, profound act of being. You, too, have an identity waiting to be discovered. It's not something you have to invent; it's already within you, like a hidden treasure. If you are already aware of what it is before reading this book, or this book has shown you even a glimpse of that truth, I urge you to hold onto it and never let go. If you haven't yet found your path, don't despair. Keep searching. Read this book again, seek out other voices of wisdom, and trust that your journey will lead you to where you're meant to be. We are all connected—different faces, different lives, but one shared essence. My story is proof that even from the depths of rejection, loss, and despair, it's possible to rise, to rediscover your purpose, and to live a life that honors your true self. So, I leave you with this: Never give up. No matter how dark the night, no matter how heavy the burden, keep moving forward. The hero within you is waiting to emerge, and the world is waiting to see the light you carry. Thank you for walking this journey with me. I look forward to meeting you someday—whether at an event, on a chance encounter, or in a moment of shared humanity. Until then, may your path be filled with discovery, resilience, and boundless joy.

God bless you.

Blurbs

Eddymufy Akhibi Eyienyien is a man of deep wisdom, resilience, and kindness. A devoted father, cherished friend, and source of inspiration, his journey began with humble beginnings, shaped by challenges that strengthened his insight and purpose. Through life's trials, he gained not only experience but a profound understanding of identity, purpose, and the courage to embrace authenticity.

In The Identity-Driven Life, Eddymufy invites readers on a deeply personal journey of self-discovery. With vulnerability and sincerity, he challenges us to look beyond societal labels, achievements, and past mistakes to uncover our true selves. Through powerful storytelling and practical wisdom, he explores themes of identity, purpose, resilience, and belief, offering guidance for those seeking clarity and fulfillment.

More than just a book, The Identity-Driven Life is a transformative guide for anyone feeling lost, uncertain, or held back by fear. Whether at a crossroads or ready to embrace their full potential, readers will find inspiration to become the person they were always meant to be.

Francette Marie Kadiri,
Author of Bag Smil og Strikponchoer

I had the pleasant opportunity to read through excerpts from Mr. Eddymufy Eyienyien's book: The Identity-Driven Life. It is not an easy task to write meaningfully about wellness and personal identity. Probably, most of the books should never have been published or bought. However, Mr. Eddymufy Eyienyien seems to succeed, and reading his writings is time well spent. He has carefully researched his field, and he has picked some very good citations to support his theories. Moreover, he definitely has a talent for writing and for communicating with his audience. I would like to wish all of his readers a thoughtful and pleasant journey

-Jens Peter Jensen
Business Strategic Consultant (Aarhus university)

About the Author

Eddy Mufy A. Eyienyien is a passionate motivational speaker, entrepreneur, and host of *The Impact Talk*, an online talk show where he invites individuals with incredible wisdom and inspiring stories to motivate others to live better, purposeful lives.

Eddy's journey is one of resilience, determination, and unshakable faith. Rejected by his father, abandoned by his mother, and raised by a grandmother suffering from a chronic spinal cord condition, he carried the weight of responsibility from a young age. Despite the hardships, he held onto his mother's dream—to see him study abroad and build a better future.

But life took an unexpected turn. At just nine years old, Eddy lost his mother, and with her, the promise of a brighter future seemed to shatter. Yet, rather than surrender to despair, he chose to fight for the dream she had envisioned for him.

With relentless determination, he embarked on a perilous journey—crossing the treacherous Sahara Desert and braving the deadly Mediterranean Sea—to reach Europe. His story is not just about survival; it is a testament to the power of perseverance, faith, and the belief that one's past does not define their future.

Beyond his speaking engagements, Eddy is also the founder of *Wise Advisor Consulting*, an enterprise dedicated to helping individuals navigate life's dilemmas, gain clarity, and make well-informed life decisions. Through his work, he continues to empower people across the world, proving that no matter the obstacles, there is always a way forward.

You can learn more about Eddymufy, and his up to date projects by visiting www.wiseadvisorconsulting.com

www.ingramcontent.com/pod-product-compliance
Lightning Source LLC
Chambersburg PA
CBHW021107130626
46554CB00002B/579